Educating Language-Minority Children

Diane August and Kenji Hakuta, *Editors*

Committee on Developing a Research Agenda
on the Education of Limited-English-Proficient
and Bilingual Students
Board on Children, Youth, and Families

Commission on Behavioral and Social Sciences and Education
National Research Council

Institute of Medicine

NATIONAL ACADEMY PRESS
Washington, D.C. 1998

NATIONAL ACADEMY PRESS • 2101 Constitution Avenue, NW • Washington, DC 20418

NOTICE: The project that is the subject of this report was approved by the Governing Board of the National Research Council, whose members are drawn from the councils of the National Academy of Sciences, the National Academy of Engineering, and the Institute of Medicine. The members of the committee responsible for the report were chosen for their special competences and with regard for appropriate balance.

This report has been reviewed by a group other than the authors according to procedures approved by a Report Review Committee consisting of members of the National Academy of Sciences, the National Academy of Engineering, and the Institute of Medicine.

This publication was supported by Purchase Order Number 43-31KV-7-D0002 between the National Academy of Sciences and the U.S. Department of Education and by the Carnegie Corporation of New York (through a grant to Stanford University). Any opinions, findings, conclusions, or recommendations expressed in this publication are those of the author(s) and do not necessarily reflect the view of the organizations or agencies that provided support for this project.

Additional copies of this report are available from:

National Academy Press
2101 Constitution Avenue, N.W.
Washington, D.C. 20418
Call 800-624-6242 or 202-334-3313 (in the Washington Metropolitan Area).
This report is also available online at http://www.nap.edu

The National Academy of Sciences is a private, nonprofit, self-perpetuating society of distinguished scholars engaged in scientific and engineering research, dedicated to the furtherance of science and technology and to their use for the general welfare. Upon the authority of the charter granted to it by the Congress in 1863, the Academy has a mandate that requires it to advise the federal government on scientific and technical matters. Dr. Bruce M. Alberts is president of the National Academy of Sciences.

The National Academy of Engineering was established in 1964, under the charter of the National Academy of Sciences, as a parallel organization of outstanding engineers. It is autonomous in its administration and in the selection of its members, sharing with the National Academy of Sciences the responsibility for advising the federal government. The National Academy of Engineering also sponsors engineering programs aimed at meeting national needs, encourages education and research, and recognizes the superior achievements of engineers. Dr. William A. Wulf is president of the National Academy of Engineering.

The Institute of Medicine was established in 1970 by the National Academy of Sciences to secure the services of eminent members of appropriate professions in the examination of policy matters pertaining to the health of the public. The Institute acts under the responsibility given to the National Academy of Sciences by its congressional charter to be an adviser to the federal government and, upon its own initiative, to identify issues of medical care, research, and education. Dr. Kenneth I. Shine is president of the Institute of Medicine.

The National Research Council was organized by the National Academy of Sciences in 1916 to associate the broad community of science and technology with the Academy's purposes of furthering knowledge and advising the federal government. Functioning in accordance with general policies determined by the Academy, the Council has become the principal operating agency of both the National Academy of Sciences and the National Academy of Engineering in providing services to the government, the public, and the scientific and engineering communities. The Council is administered jointly by both Academies and the Institute of Medicine. Dr. Bruce M. Alberts and Dr. William A. Wulf are chairman and vice chairman, respectively, of the National Research Council.

Contents

PREFACE   ix

1   OVERVIEW   1
Purpose and Scope of the Report, 2
Terminology, 3
Background, 4
Organization of the Report, 9

2   BILINGUALISM AND SECOND-LANGUAGE LEARNING   11
Findings, 11
Implications, 19

3   COGNITIVE ASPECTS OF SCHOOL LEARNING:
LITERACY DEVELOPMENT AND CONTENT LEARNING   21
Findings, 21
Implications, 30

4   THE SOCIAL CONTEXT OF SCHOOL LEARNING   33
Findings, 33
Implications, 37

5   STUDENT ASSESSMENT   41
    Findings, 42
    Implications, 51

6   PROGRAM EVALUATION   55
    Findings, 55
    Implications, 70

7   STUDIES OF SCHOOL AND CLASSROOM
    EFFECTIVENESS   73
    Findings, 73
    Implications, 85
    Appendix, 87

CONCLUDING REMARKS   89

REFERENCES   91

BIOGRAPHICAL SKETCHES OF COMMITTEE
MEMBERS AND STAFF   113

OTHER REPORTS FROM THE BOARD ON CHILDREN,
YOUTH, AND FAMILIES   118

Preface

This short volume summarizes portions of a much longer report entitled *Improving Schooling for Language-Minority Children: A Research Agenda*, published in 1997. The longer report was the work of the Committee on Developing a Research Agenda on the Education of Limited-English-Proficient and Bilingual Students, established under the auspices of the Board on Children, Youth, and Families of the Commission on Behavioral and Social Sciences and Education (CBASSE) of the National Research Council (NRC) and the Institute of Medicine (IOM). Eleven experts—representing the areas of language, cognitive, and child development; bilingual and multicultural education; education evaluation; assessment; and educational history—reviewed and discussed existing research relevant to the education of English-language learners and bilingual students and made recommendations for the next generation of research. In addition to the substantive areas, the committee investigated issues surrounding the infrastructure for research in this field and made recommendations for its improvement.

Whereas the first report makes recommendations for the next generation of research and improvements in the research infrastructure, this report was written for educators and policymakers. As such, it summarizes information in the first report that is likely to be of most interest to this audience—research findings on bilingualism and second-language learning, the cognitive aspects of school learning, the social context of school learning, student assessment, program evaluation, and school and classroom effectiveness. In addition, it considers the implications for educational practice of these disparate domains of research.

The committee wishes to acknowledge the support of the National Institute on the Education of At-Risk Students, the Office for Educational Research and Improvement at the U.S. Department of Education, and the Carnegie Corporation of New York (through a grant to Stanford University) for the preparation of this summary report. Support for preparation of the full report on which this summary is based was provided by several offices within the U.S. Department of Education—the Office of Bilingual Education and Minority Language Affairs, the Office of the Under Secretary, and the Office of Educational Research and Improvement. Funding was also provided by the Spencer Foundation, the Carnegie Corporation of New York, the Pew Charitable Trusts, the John D. and Catherine T. MacArthur Foundation, and the Andrew W. Mellon Foundation (through a grant to Stanford University).

Several commissioned papers contributed to this report. We thank Luis Moll, Rosi Andrade, and Norma Gonzalez for "Rethinking Culture, Community and Schooling: Implications for the Education of Bilingual Students"; Patton Tabors for "Second Language Acquisition and Preschool Education: Research Findings, Methods, Implications, and Future Directions"; Claude Goldenberg for "Effective Schooling for LEP Students: The School Domain"; and Nitza Hidalgo for "Parental and Community Involvement in the Education of Limited English Proficient and Bilingual Students."

The committee benefited from the support of staff from the Division of Social Sciences: Faith Mitchell provided ongoing advice and encouragement; Janine Bilyeu and Carole Spalding provided administrative assistance; and Rona Briere, as editor, contributed to the presentation of the committee's views.

Diane August, *Study Director*
Kenji Hakuta, *Chair*
Committee on Developing a Research Agenda
on the Education of Limited-English-Proficient
and Bilingual Students

1

Overview

American education has, until recently, focused primarily on meeting the needs of native English-speaking children. However, a large and growing number of students in U.S. schools come from homes where the language background is other than English. These limited-English-proficient (LEP) students are overwhelmingly from families with low incomes and lower levels of formal education. Thirty years ago these students were expected to "sink or swim" in a school environment that did not pay particular attention to their linguistic background.

This approach continued until just a few decades ago, when the proportion of LEP students began to increase substantially. Since the 1970s, a variety of educational approaches to meeting the needs of English-language learners have been tried.[1] These approaches are designed to help these students develop proficiency in English, as well as learn the knowledge and skills that make up the curriculum. Impetus for these programs has come from a number of sources: Congress, the courts, state legislatures, departments of education, and various professional and advocacy groups. At first, these programs were not based on research, but

---

[1]Throughout this report, the committee has elected wherever possible to use the term "English-language learners" (proposed by Rivera [1994]) rather than the term "LEP students." The committee feels that the former is a positive term, whereas the latter assigns a negative label. Moreover, we have chosen to forego the editorially convenient practice of reducing English-language learners to an acronym.

relied on professional intuitions, political voices, and a moral conviction that something had to be done to reverse the pattern of poor academic outcomes for these students. What little research existed focused on middle- and upper-middle-class Cuban exiles, populations of a different cultural background and generally of higher socioeconomic status than today's typical English-language learner.

Beginning in the early 1970s and continuing to the present, a research base bearing on English-language learners has been built in response to a number of circumstances. Major developments in basic research, especially in the areas of language and cognitive development, followed on the heels of the cognitive revolution of the 1960s and stimulated such research on English-language learners. The political controversy over bilingual education (i.e., use of a native language other than English in instruction) led to a line of research aimed at evaluating the comparative effectiveness of bilingual education and other approaches using only English. Simultaneously, general concern with educational effectiveness stimulated research aimed at identifying characteristics of "effective" schools, and this in turn stimulated parallel work to identify characteristics of effective programs for English-language learners. These and other developments have resulted in a rich portfolio of research that is relevant to the education of English-language learners, ranging from basic processes to program evaluation and program characteristics research.

Almost 30 years after congressional passage of the Bilingual Education Act as Title VII of the Stafford-Hawkins Elementary and Secondary Education Act, we are now in a position to take stock of what we know.

PURPOSE AND SCOPE OF THE REPORT

The purpose of this report is to review and summarize the current state of knowledge that has been or could be applied to the education of students who are not fully English proficient. We have endeavored to move beyond the narrow focus on language of instruction that has dominated education and policy discussions to examine individual, social, and instructional factors that bear on student learning.

In its full report, the committee reviews research in a broad range of substantive areas. This summary version focuses on a subset of these areas: bilingualism and second-language learning, literacy development and content learning, the social context of school learning, student assessment, program evaluation, and school and classroom effectiveness. We note that children develop and learn in families, in neighborhoods, and in societies, as well as in classrooms and schools. There is ample evidence that each of these contexts influences child development and academic achievement. For English-language learners, the important contextual issues include poverty, which is common among these students; attendance in underfunded schools; low social status accorded to members of certain ethnic and immigrant groups; familial stress; low teacher expectations; and the child's need to adjust to novel school practices of language use, behavioral appropriateness, and ways of learning. In the interest of brevity, these larger contextual issues are not directly or fully addressed in this report, but form the foundation for the issues that are examined.

Classrooms and schools, too, exist within complex environments, such as local and state systems; they are also influenced by federal policy, the media, and public opinion. A description of these contexts and factors and analysis of their impact on the education of English-language learners deserves serious attention by researchers. However, this committee saw these areas as lying mostly beyond its charge.

A final contextual parameter for this report is a set of assumptions shared by the members of the committee. They are as follows: (1) all children in the United States should be able to function fully in the English language; (2) English-language learners should be held to the same expectations and have the same opportunities for achievement in academic content areas as other students; and (3) in an increasingly global economic and political world, proficiency in languages other than English and an understanding of different cultures are valuable in their own right, and should be among the major goals for schools.

TERMINOLOGY

There are many labels for the students who come from language backgrounds other than English and whose English proficiency is not yet developed to the point where they can profit fully from English-only instruction. We have elected to use the term proposed by Rivera (1994)—English-language learners. We use the term "LEP" when quoting another source, when citing such things as legal requirements, and when referring to issues rather than to children.

Two other terms appear frequently in this report:

• Bilingual students—We use the term bilingual to refer to an individual with a language background other than English who has developed proficiency in his or her primary language and enough proficiency in English not to be disadvantaged in an English-only school environment.

• Language-minority students—This term refers to individuals from homes where a language other than English is actively used, who therefore have had an opportunity to develop some level of proficiency in a language other than English. A language-minority student may be of limited English proficiency, bilingual, or primarily monolingual in English.

BACKGROUND

This section provides background information on the student population of English-language learners, the types of programs designed to meet their needs, the teachers of these students, and the means used to measure educational outcomes for this population.

Students

According to a nationally representative sample of school districts, the number of English-language learners in grades K-12 in the fall of 1991 was 2,314,079 (Fleischman and Hopstock, 1993, hereafter referred to as the Descriptive Study). This number represents an increase of almost 1 million students over the results of a survey conducted in 1984 using similar methodology.[2] Other estimates of the English-language learner population have ranged from 2.0 to 3.3 million because of the varying estimation methods used (Hopstock and Bucaro, 1993).

By far the largest proportion of English-language learners are native speakers of Spanish (73 percent). This is followed by Vietnamese (3.9 percent); Hmong (1.8 percent); Cantonese (1.7 percent); Cambodian (1.6 percent); Korean (1.6 percent); Laotian (1.3 percent); Navajo (1.3 percent); Tagalog (1.3 percent); and Russian, French Creole, Arabic, Portuguese, Japanese, Armenian, Chinese (unspecified), Mandarin, Farsi, Hindi, and Polish (Fleischman and Hopstock, 1993).

Geographically speaking, English-language learners are concentrated in a small number of large states. Of all the language-minority individuals enumerated in the 1990 census, 67 percent resided in just five states: California (30 percent), Texas (15 percent), New York (11 percent), Florida (6 percent), and Illinois (5 percent). Relatively high proportions of English-language learners are found in a small number of districts; in 1991, for example, 6 percent of districts served a student population that was at least 40 percent English-language learners (Descriptive Study).

---

[2]Some of this increase is probably due to improvements in methods for identification and reporting of English-language learners.

Recently, however, as the number of immigrants has increased, some have moved to smaller cities and suburban and rural areas, as well as to regions that have had few language minorities in the past, such as the midwest. This trend has been stimulated by a desire for employment and a lower cost of living (*Education Week*, September 11, 1996).

Most English-language learners are in the early elementary grades. Over half (53 percent) can be found in grades K-4. They make up a decreasing proportion of the total population in these grades: 8 percent of all kindergartners, down to about 6 percent of fourth graders.

As suggested earlier, English-language learners are also overwhelmingly from disadvantaged socioeconomic backgrounds. For example, 77 percent of English-language learners were eligible for free or reduced-price lunches, compared with 38 percent overall in the same schools. According to another study, known as Prospects (a Congressionally mandated evaluation of Chapter 1/Title I that follows longitudinally a nationally representative sample of students [Moss and Puma, 1995]), a large percentage of English-language learners attend schools where a high proportion (75-100 percent) of the other students are in poverty—43 percent of first grade and 51 percent of third grade English-language learners attend such schools, compared with about 13 percent of the overall population.

There are important differences between Hispanic and non-Hispanic language-minority groups. An analysis of the Current Population Survey from 1989 shows substantial family income differences within the non-English-language groups (McArthur, 1993). For example, 35 percent of families that spoke Asian/Pacific Island languages had incomes under $20,000, compared with 57 percent for Spanish speakers. There were parallel differences in parental educational attainment.

Program Definitions

The major dimensions used to define educational programs for English-language learners relate to native-language use, the mix of the students' linguistic backgrounds, and the goals of the program. However, most surveys of actual program characteristics show wide variation even within given nomenclatures. In addition, approaches do not exist in isolation, coexist even within schools, and are often combined in various ways, depending on the availability of staff and resources. With these constraints in mind, we offer the following generic program labels and definitions. Note that the first two definitions refer to instructional approaches for teaching English based on English as a second language

(ESL), while the last four are program models that are designed to meet the needs of English-language learners more broadly, and may include those ESL approaches:

• ESL—Students receive specified periods of instruction aimed at the development of English-language skills, with a primary focus on grammar, vocabulary, and communication rather than academic content.
• Content-based ESL—Students receive specified periods of ESL instruction that is structured around academic content rather than generic English-language skills.
• Sheltered instruction—Students receive subject matter instruction in English, modified so that it is understandable to them at their levels of English proficiency.
• Structured immersion—All students in the program are English-language learners, usually, though not always, from different language backgrounds. They receive instruction in English, with an attempt made to adjust the level of English so subject matter is comprehensible. Typically there is no native-language support.
• Transitional bilingual education—Most students in the program are English-language learners. They receive some degree of instruction in the native language; however, the goal of the program is to transition to English as quickly as possible, so that even within the program, there is a shift toward using primarily English.
• Maintenance bilingual education—Most students in the program are English-language learners and from the same language background. They receive significant amounts of their instruction in their native language. Unlike transitional programs, however, these programs continue native language instruction even as students' English proficiency increases because their aim is to develop academic proficiency in both English and the native language.
• Two-way bilingual programs—A portion of the students (ideally half) in these programs are native speakers of English, and the others are English-language learners from the same language group. The goal of the program is to develop proficiency in both languages for both groups of students.

Data on program types are difficult to collect and interpret because program philosophy and objectives do not always translate into program practice. However, it is safe to say that ESL-only (with some variants of content-based ESL and sheltered instruction) and transitional bilingual education are the two prevalent models for educating English-language learners. A recent study found over 1600 schools that reported offering content-based ESL and/or sheltered instruction (Sheppard, 1995). Structured immersion programs are very few in number, as evidenced by the fact that a recent study examining the effects of structured immersion (Ramirez et al., 1991) had to select all programs found. Maintenance programs are also relatively rare, and although two-way bilingual programs are becoming increasingly popular, a recent survey identified just 182 schools nationwide where this method is used (Christian and Whitcher, 1995).

The Descriptive Study examined factors that predicted which services involving native-language use were provided by schools. The strongest predictors were the availability of teachers who spoke the native (non-English) language and the percentage of English-language learners whose native language was Spanish. School poverty level was positively related to the likelihood of English-language learners' receiving instruction in their native language. Among the first grade cohort in the Prospects study, 70 percent of those in high-poverty schools received some math instruction in their native language, compared with 17 percent for those in medium- and low-poverty schools.

The Teachers

The Descriptive Study found that approximately 15 percent of all public school teachers in the country had at least one English-language learner in their class. About 66 percent of teachers serving English-language learners were mainstream classroom teachers serving some of these students; about 18 percent were mainstream classroom teachers serving these students primarily. The study also found (p. 39) that most "teachers of English-language learners hold regular elementary and secondary teaching certification; only small percentages are certified in bilingual education (10 percent) or ESL (8 percent)." About 42 percent of teachers of English-language learners spoke a non-English language that was the native language of one or more of those students. The study also found that only 55 percent of the teachers of English-language learners had taken relevant college courses or had received recent inservice professional development relating to the instruction of these students.

Educational Outcomes

Data on educational outcomes are particularly difficult to obtain for the English-language learner population because their limited English proficiency hampers valid use of achievement measures administered in English.[3] Many English-language learners were eliminated from national data sets such as the National Assessment of Educational Progress (NAEP) and the National Educational Longitudinal Study (NELS) because they were thought to be insufficiently proficient in English to complete the questionnaires or take the tests. Thus, any estimate based on the sample of English-language learners who took the tests would likely be biased toward those most proficient in English.

The Prospects study provides some measure of achievement in the early grades. Results of the Comprehensive Test of Basic Skills (CTBS) showed English-language learners performing considerably below general population norms in both reading and math when tested in English. For example, the third grade cohort achieved at a mean percentile level of 24.8 percent in reading and 35.2 percent in math, compared with 56.4 and 56.8 percent, respectively, for all public school students. For those students who took the SABE, a similar test administered in Spanish, the mean percentile was somewhat but not much better, at 41.1 percent for reading and 35.2 percent for math. For both measures, performance was strongly related to the concentration of students from poor families in the school. The higher the concentration of poor families, the worse the student performance, whereas the performance of English-language learners in schools with school poverty concentrations of 20-34 percent was not substantially different from the general population norm for all public school students. However, although there is an effect of poverty, limited English proficiency also plays a role in low performance, as indicated by substantially lower scores for English-language learners as compared with language-minority students (not currently limited-English-proficient) in high-poverty schools.

Prospects also examined student grades and teacher ratings of student ability and social and affective characteristics. English-language learners were less likely than other students to receive grades of "excellent" in reading or math. Moreover, teachers rated such students lower than other students in their overall ability to perform in school and their overall achievement in school. However, teachers did not judge English-language learners to be different on a number of affective characteristics, such as honesty, friendliness, happiness, self-esteem, ability to get along with teachers, and respect for authority. There were also no differences

---

[3]Recently, the National Center for Educational Statistics has made efforts to incorporate more of these students in its assessments (see Chapters 5 and 9 of the full report).

from the overall student population in school attendance, tardiness, and school suspensions.

Finally, drop-out rates for language-minority students provide one important indicator of educational outcomes for English-language learners. Data from the 1989 Current Population Survey show that 31.3 percent of native Spanish speakers aged 16 to 24 were not enrolled in and had not completed high school, compared with 10.5 percent of English-only speakers. Figures for the other language groups were comparable to those for the English-only speakers. The difference between the Spanish-speaking and other language-minority groups is largely eliminated when one controls statistically for parental educational attainment (McArthur, 1993:Table 16).

To summarize, available data on student outcomes indicate distressing results for English-language learners—both in the short-term outcomes of test scores and teacher judgments and in longer-term outcomes such as high school completion rates. Furthermore, other confounding factors—poverty level and level of parental educational attainment—are strongly related to lower achievement.

ORGANIZATION OF THE REPORT

The remainder of this report is organized partly around the traditional distinction between basic and applied research, but also is structured to reflect specific areas of concern for educational practitioners and policymakers. The three chapters to follow (Chapters 2-4) summarize research findings on bilingualism, second-language acquisition, literacy, content area learning, the social context of school learning, and intergroup relations. The next three chapters summarize the findings of more applied research: student assessment (Chapter 5), program evaluation (Chapter 6), and school and classroom effectiveness (Chapter 7). These topics were selected because they represent key areas of concern in the current dialogue on educational reform. Each chapter begins with a summary of key findings and ends with a section on educational and research implications. It should be noted that the research questions posed in the latter sections are intended to be addressed by practicing educators and policymakers, in addition to researchers.

Differing research traditions (cognitive aspects of school learning, program evaluation, and research on school and classroom effectiveness) are treated separately in individual chapters so the reader can get a sense of how the evidence from each tradition or data source is analyzed and how inferences are drawn. However, it should be noted that there is some overlap among the kinds of studies cited in individual chapters.

BILINGUALISM AND SECOND-LANGUAGE LEARNING:
KEY FINDINGS

A review of the literature on bilingualism and second-language learning reveals the following key findings:

- Bilingualism is pervasive throughout the world; there is nothing unusual about it. It varies according to the conditions under which people become bilingual, the uses they have for their various languages, and the social status of the languages. For example, some children learn two languages from the onset of language acquisition, while others begin to acquire a second language when they arrive in school.
- Bilingualism shows no negative effects on the overall linguistic, cognitive, or social development of children, and may even provide general advantages in these areas of mental functioning.
- Second-language acquisition is a complex process because language is so central to human functioning. For example, second-language learning can be viewed as a linguistic and cognitive accomplishment, but social variables also affect language use and structure.
- An important dimension of second-language acquisition is the age and concomitant cognitive skills of the second-language learner. Because of their more advanced cognitive skills, older children acquire a second language at a more rapid rate than younger children.
- Second-language abilities should be assessed in relation to the uses of language the learner will require, rather than in isolation as an abstract competence.
- Individual and group factors such as age of learning, intelligence, attitudes, and personality have been examined in hopes of explaining individual differences in language learning. Age of learning and intelligence are related to certain aspects of second-language acquisition, but attitudes and personality are not promising explanations.
- Many bilinguals in the United States show a strong preference for English in most conversational situations, and this shift in preference from the native language to English results in a monolingual English upbringing for their children.
- Evidence from preschool programs reviewed in this chapter suggests that use of the child's native language does not impede the acquisition of English.

2

Bilingualism and
Second-Language Learning

This chapter provides a broad overview of the findings from research on bilingualism and second-language learning, including types of bilingualism, linguistic aspects of second-language acquisition, language shift, and classroom environments for second-language learning. Further, it analyzes the implications of these findings for the education of English-language learners in the United States. By necessity, a broad overview of these rich traditions involves a high level of synthesis. This review draws liberally from several existing syntheses, which can be consulted for further details (Baetens-Beardsmore, 1986; Bialystok and Hakuta, 1994; Grosjean, 1982; Hakuta, 1986; Hamers and Blanc, 1989; Klein, 1986; Larsen-Freeman and Long, 1990; McLaughlin, 1984, 1985; and Romaine, 1995).

FINDINGS

This review begins by distinguishing the various types of bilingualism. It then briefly examines the consequences of bilingualism. The third section looks at linguistic aspects of acquiring a second language, while the fourth addresses individual differences in second-language acquisition. Language shift—in which ethnic minority groups shift their primary language to that of the dominant majority—is then examined. The final section reviews findings on educational conditions for second-language learning.

Types of Bilingualism

Bilingualism is pervasive throughout the world, but there is consider-able variation in (1) the conditions under which people become bilingual, (2) the uses they have for their various languages, and (3) the societal status of the languages. For example, in postcolonial Africa, students may be educated in English or French while another language is spoken in the home, and yet another (e.g., Swahili in eastern Africa) may be used in public encounters and institutional settings, such as the courts (Fishman, 1978). In officially bilingual countries such as Switzerland, children use one language at home and for most schooling, but are expected to acquire competence in at least one other official language; thus in Switzerland, French and German are of equivalent social status and importance to success. Yet another set of conditions is created in bilingual households, where parents who are native speakers of two different languages choose to use both in the home. Finally, in other contexts bilingualism is often the product of migration. Immigrants frequently continue to use their native language—which may be of low status and not institutionally sup-ported—at home, and learn the dominant language of their new society only as required for work, public encounters, or schooling. The children of such families may end up fully bilingual, bilingual with the new lan-guage dominant, or having little knowledge of the parental language. They are the children of particular interest in this report.

A number of typologies of bilingualism follow. A major distinction among these typologies is that some focus their explanation of second-language acquisition at the individual and others at the societal level.

Individual Level

Weinreich (1953) theorized a distinction among compound, coordi-nate, and subordinate bilinguals, who differ in the way words in their languages relate to underlying concepts. In the compound form, the two languages represent the same concept, whereas in the coordinate form, the concepts themselves are independent and parallel. In the subordinate form, the weaker language is represented through the stronger language.

Researchers also distinguish at the individual level between simulta-neous and sequential bilingualism: the former begins from the onset of language acquisition, while the latter begins after about age 5, when the basic components of first-language knowledge are in place (McLaughlin, 1984). In the sequential type, a distinction is made between early and late bilinguals, according to the age at which second-language acquisition occurred (Genesee et al., 1978).

Later in this report we discuss whether different types of education programs might result in qualitatively different types of individual bilinguals. Findings suggest, by and large, that bilingualism attained under different conditions of exposure will not differ in the ways language is organized with respect to cognitive structures.

Social Level

Typologies of bilingualism based on societal variables have focused mainly on the prestige and status of the languages involved. Fishman et al. (1966) draw a distinction between "folk" and "elite" bilingualism, referring to the social status of the bilingual group. The "folk" are immigrants and linguistic minorities who exist within the milieu of a dominant language that is not their own and whose own language is not held in high esteem within the society. The "elite" are those who speak the dominant language and whose societal status is enhanced through the mastery of additional languages. As Fishman observes, "Many Americans have long been of the opinion that bilingualism is 'a good thing' if it was acquired via travel (preferably to Paris) or via formal education (preferably at Harvard) but that it is a 'bad thing' if it was acquired from one's immigrant parents or grandparents" (pp. 122-123).

Similarly, Lambert (1975) distinguishes "additive" from "subtractive" bilingualism. This distinction relates to the effect of learning a second language on the retention of the native language. In additive bilingualism, the native language is secure, and the second language serves as an enrichment. Canadian French immersion programs for the English-speaking majority are a prime example of additive bilingualism since native English speakers maintain their English and add French. In subtractive bilingualism, the native language is less robust; society assumes that it will be used only temporarily until replaced by the dominant language as the group assimilates. Most immigrants to the United States, Canada, and Australia experience subtractive bilingualism; their skills in their native languages erode over time, and English becomes their dominant language (see also the discussion of language shift later in this chapter).

These broader social distinctions help explain why programs that seem quite similar can have such divergent effects in different social settings— for example, why an immersion program in Canada succeeds in teaching French to English-speaking students who continue to maintain full proficiency in English and to function at a high academic level, while an immersion program to teach English to Spanish-speaking immigrants in the United States often results in both a shift to monolingualism in English and academic failure.

Consequences of Bilingualism

A commonly expressed fear about childhood bilingualism is that it could confuse the child, both linguistically and cognitively. However, Peal and Lambert (1962), widely credited for introducing important controls in studies that compare monolinguals with bilinguals, describe a bilingual child as "a youngster whose wider experiences in two cultures have given him advantages which a monolingual does not enjoy. Intellectually his experience with two language systems seems to have left him with a mental flexibility, a superiority in concept formation, a more diversified set of mental abilities" (p. 20). The results of other studies have typically supported Peal and Lambert's claims that bilingual groups are superior on a variety of measures of cognitive skill, such as nonverbal reasoning and awareness of language structure (Duncan and DeAvila, 1979; Galambos and Hakuta, 1988; Hakuta, 1987; see Reynolds, 1991, for a review).

Another tradition of research comes from case studies of individual children exposed to two languages at home. Generally, these studies (Ronjat, 1913; Leopold, 1939, 1947, 1949a, 1949b) suggest that children can become productive bilinguals in a variety of language-use settings, though exposure to a language for less than 20 hours a week does not seem sufficient for a child to produce words in that language, at least up to age 3 (Pearson et al., 1997). Very few cases of what might be considered language confusion are reported.

Linguistic Aspects of Second-Language Acquisition

The theoretical and empirical work in second-language acquisition serves as the basis for defining what one means by "proficiency" in a second language. Some researchers have defined it narrowly around the control of grammatical rules, others around the ability to use language in accomplishing cognitive tasks, and still others around the social and communicative aspects of language.

What is clear is that second-language acquisition is a complex process requiring a diverse set of explanatory factors (Bialystok and Hakuta, 1994). Developing an inclusive theory of how a second language is acquired necessitates both the description of how specific domains of proficiency are acquired and an explanation of how acquisition mechanisms work together to produce the integrated knowledge of a language that enables its use for communication. An important conclusion that is shared by all research perspectives is the rejection of behaviorist theories of language that emphasize the role of variables such as frequency of occurrence, time on task, and the motivational state of the learner in shaping the learning process.

A second important dimension of second-language acquisition is the extent of involvement of the native language in the acquisition process. Today most researchers believe language transfer plays a role in second-language acquisition (Bialystok and Hakuta, 1994; Odlin, 1989), perhaps being more evident in the quantitative (speed of acquisition) rather than qualitative (e.g., types of errors and patterns of acquisition) aspects of the process (Odlin, 1989). That is, it takes longer to learn a language that is typologically very different from the native language than one that is relatively similar. For example, it would be easier for a native English speaker to learn French than Chinese.

A third dimension of importance in the acquisition of a second language is the age and concomitant cognitive skills of the second-language learner. These and other factors are discussed in the next section.

Individual Differences in Second-Language Acquisition

The most striking fact about second-language learning, especially as compared with first-language learning, is the variability in outcomes. Many individual and group variables have been examined in attempts to explain success or failure in second-language acquisition.

Age of Learning

One frequently cited factor is the age of the learner, with the assumption that younger learners acquire a second language more quickly and with a higher level of proficiency. Periodic reviews of this literature (Bialystok and Hakuta, 1994; Collier, 1987; Epstein et al., 1996; Harley and Wang, 1997; Krashen et al., 1982; Long, 1990; Snow, 1987) have not supported this claim very well. Supporters of the critical period for second-language acquisition frequently refer to the literature on first-language acquisition, such as studies of children with severe and extreme linguistic isolation in early childhood. It is important to note that even though there may be a critical period in the learning of a first language, this does not necessarily imply that there is such a period for learning additional languages.

The research provides no clear-cut answers to guide decisions on when English should be taught because younger learners do not necessarily acquire a second language more quickly than older learners. Individual differences account for this variation. For example, children with weak first-language skills will not acquire their second language as quickly as those with more developed skills (Cummins, 1984; Hakuta, 1987).

Intelligence

Another factor in second-language acquisition may be general intelligence. This factor has been studied mainly in the arena of foreign-language learning in the classroom (Carroll, 1986; Gardner, 1983; Oller, 1981). For immigrant learners and those in immersion settings, research findings suggest that second-language learning is not impeded by learning disabilities or low intelligence to the extent it would be in formal learning settings such as classrooms (Bruck, 1982, 1984; see Genesee, 1992, for a review). In the field of bilingual education, second-language acquisition has not been tied to questions of general aptitude, although educational practitioners commonly observe that second-language acquisition is easier for students with a history of formal education and higher socioeconomic backgrounds. Furthermore, correlational studies examining relative proficiencies in the two languages of bilingual children show that native-language proficiency is a strong predictor of second-language development (Cummins, 1984; Hakuta, 1987).

Attitudes

It is clear that attitude and motivation are important factors in second-language learning in some contexts, such as for students who are studying a foreign language in the classroom. Yet the few studies that have looked at the importance of these factors in the acquisition of English among immigrants to the United States have had largely negative findings. For example, Hakuta and D'Andrea (1992) found that Mexican-American attitudes toward English and Spanish did not predict English proficiency. In sociolinguistic settings such as the United States, it is likely that any variation in the attitudes of immigrant populations toward English will be largely overridden by the overwhelming importance of English to getting ahead in the society.

Personality

Many studies have attempted to isolate factors related to individual predisposition, over and above basic intelligence, toward second-language acquisition. Most of this work is focused on learning a foreign language rather than on learning a language in the society where it is used. Given the inordinate difficulty of validly measuring personality constructs cross-culturally, this is probably not a very fruitful area for future research, although it will continue to be a source of speculation because of its intrinsic interest.

Language Shift

Language shift occurs when an ethnic group gradually changes its preference and use of language from its original ethnic language to the sociologically dominant language. The evidence for a rapid shift to English among immigrants in the United States is well noted (Lieberson et al., 1975). The shift from non-English to English may occur both intra-individually and intergenerationally. That is, during the course of their lifetime, individuals shift their primary-language preference from their native language to English, and ethnolinguistic communities in successive generations likewise shift their linguistic preference. Ethnographic studies, as well as large-scale demographic information (Fishman et al., 1966; Lopez, 1978; Veltman, 1983), suggest that bilinguals in the United States show a strong preference for English in many conversational situations and that this preference is translated into a monolingual English upbringing for their offspring. In addition, although the consistent choice of English can lead to increased proficiency in English, it also leads to decreased proficiency in the native language, even for an adult speaker (Seliger and Vago, 1991).

Classroom Environments and Second-Language Learning

This section reviews studies on classroom environments and their relationship to second-language learning. Researchers have examined recurring features of classroom interaction hypothesized to be relevant to students' development of a second language (van Lier, 1988; Ellis, 1984). Others have begun to offer detailed pictures of how the student's two languages are used in elementary-grade bilingual classrooms (e.g.,

Enright, 1982; Milk, 1990; Shultz, 1975). These studies generally do not link classroom communication and the learning of linguistic features or report outcome data with respect to English acquisition or native-language development. However, they have clarified what might be meant by comprehensible input[1] (Krashen, 1982; Long, 1983; Pica, 1987) and have shown that English tends to predominate in most classrooms in terms of messages conveyed and frequency of use.

Other studies have looked more generally at the effects of English-only and bilingual school environments on the overall language and cognitive development of English-language learners. Paul and Jarvis (1992), for example, compared English-language learners in bilingual and monolingual prekindergarten classrooms, and found positive outcomes for the children in the bilingual classrooms on a criterion-referenced test, the Chicago Early Assessment and Remediation Laboratory (EARLY). An evaluation study of the Carpinteria Preschool Program, in which classroom activities were carried out exclusively in Spanish, shows similarly positive effects of first-language use on second-language acquisition (Campos, 1995).

Such studies point to the importance of understanding the linguistic environments of institutional settings that serve as the primary base for second-language acquisition. It is critically important to understand preschool environments for two major reasons. First, during the preschool years, language development itself is a major outcome of interest. The few studies reviewed suggest that the development of the native language and of English for English-language learners are interdependent—that programs to develop the native language also serve to promote the acquisition of English (Ramirez et al., 1991)—but additional work is needed in this area. Second, there are increasing calls for the expansion of high-quality preschool opportunities for all children (e.g., Carnegie Corporation, 1996). A critical ingredient in defining quality is the linguistic environment of these programs. This represents a window of opportunity for research to make a difference for a large number of programs and children.

---

[1]Comprehensible input might be equated with adjustments similar to those parents make when talking with young children, such as organizing talk around visible referents, using gestures, using simple syntax, producing many repetitions and paraphrases, speaking slowly and clearly, checking often for comprehension, and expanding on and extending topics introduced by the learner.

IMPLICATIONS

Educational

All English-language learners acquire English. However, there is considerable variation in the rate of second-language acquisition due to individual and societal factors. Individual factors that promote second-language acquisition include a history of formal education and higher socioeconomic background, the extent of native-language proficiency, and similarity between the student's native language and the language being acquired.

Bilingualism, far from impeding the child's overall cognitive or linguistic development, leads to positive growth in these areas. Programs whose goals are to promote bilingualism should do so without fear of negative consequences. English-language learners who develop their native-language proficiency do not compromise their acquisition of English.

The social climate in the United States overwhelmingly results in the dominance of English and quickly restricts the native languages of immigrants to a limited range of uses, and usually only to the first generation. Any language policy or program that attempts to develop bilingualism will have to take these larger societal trends into consideration.

Research

Although we have some research-based information on individual and group factors that account for variation in second-language acquisition, more work is needed, particularly on group factors. An important contribution to understanding variability in second-language acquisition would be an enhanced understanding of the components of English proficiency and how these components interact. Also important is the question of how proficiencies in the two languages of bilinguals are interrelated and how language and other domains of human functioning interact.

Assessment of second-language learners should involve analysis of unstructured, spontaneous speech in addition to more structured instruments. An important research goal is thus to create a common pool of spontaneous speech data for use by researchers.

Macro-level questions about language shift in the United States have amply demonstrated the short-lived nature of non-English languages. Research is also needed to help understand the dynamics of language shift.

COGNITIVE ASPECTS OF SCHOOL LEARNING: KEY FINDINGS

Research to date on the cognitive aspects of how children acquire literacy and content area knowledge in school has yielded the following key findings:

- Future successful readers typically arrive at school with a set of prior experiences and well-established skills conducive to literacy, including an understanding of literacy, abstract knowledge of the sound and structure of language, a certain level of vocabulary development, and oral connected discourse skills. In terms of English-language learners, there is considerable variability among ethnic or language groups in home literacy practices; some minimal ability to segment spoken language into phonemic units is a prerequisite to beginning to read, and bilingualism promotes this ability; English vocabulary is a primary determinant of reading comprehension; and there are positive correlations between English second-language oral proficiency and reading ability, particularly at higher grade levels, but not equally across all first-language groups.

- Early instruction is impacted by lack of explicit instruction in the local orthography, absence of background knowledge and skills acquired in highly literate environments, and lack of semantic support for decoding that comes from familiarity with the words one reads. With regard to reading instruction in a second language, there is remarkably little direct relevant research.

- Studies of the nature of what can be transferred from first- to second-language reading need to take into account not only the level of first-language reading, but also the level and content of the second-language reading material.

- English-language learners may encounter difficulties in reading because of limited access to word meanings in English and novel rhetorical structures.

- Different subjects have different core structures; there are multiple kinds of knowledge—knowledge of ideas and facts, as well as knowledge of how to do something; and prior knowledge plays a significant role in learning.

- The above five conclusions suggest that literacy assessments alone are not adequate measures for understanding specific subject matter knowledge; certain disciplines may lend themselves more easily to the transfer of knowledge across languages, depending on the structure of knowledge within the domain; studies of the subject matter specificity of learning and issues surrounding different classes of knowledge suggest the difficulty of providing high-quality instruction designed for English-language learners; and the way content learned in one language is accessed in a second is of concern since depth, interconnectness, and accessibility of prior knowledge dramatically influence the processing of new information.

3

Cognitive Aspects of School Learning: Literacy Development and Content Learning

English-language learners in the United States are overrepresented among those performing poorly in school. An understanding of the cognitive challenges posed by learning to read and by acquiring new content knowledge, whether in a first or a second language, is a prerequisite to designing better instruction for these and indeed all children. Whereas the previous chapter focused primarily on acquisition of oral language skills, the focus in this chapter is on reading, writing, and subject matter knowledge. The emphasis is on research on the cognitive nature of the challenges inherent in learning to read or learning subjects such as math or history, and on the factors that facilitate success in learning. Most of this research has been conducted with monolingual native English-speaking children, but nonetheless is relevant to English-language learners. It should be noted that although this chapter includes some discussion of optimal instruction in the area of reading, most of the discussion regarding instruction is included in Chapter 7, on studies of school and classroom effectiveness.

FINDINGS

Literacy Development

There has been a vast amount of research related to literacy and literacy instruction. Here we can only provide examples of what has been learned in the various domains of literacy development, focusing on concepts that are relatively well established for first-language reading and their potential relevance for understanding literacy development among English-language learners. We examine in turn prerequisites for the successful acquisition of reading skills, optimal early reading instruction, reading as a developmental process, and the comprehension of skilled readers.

Prerequisites for the Successful Acquisition of Reading

It is clear that future successful readers typically arrive at school with a set of prior experiences and well-established skills conducive to literacy. The findings in this area are fairly consistent, though explanations of how those prerequisites function to foster literacy development are not. The key prerequisites include an understanding of the notion of literacy (both as a social process and as specific knowledge about letters, language, and symbolic systems that are prerequisites to full literacy); an abstract knowledge of the sound and structure of language (the ability to segment language into phonemic units, such as rhyming or focusing on similarities in sound rather than in meaning when grouping words); a certain level of vocabulary development; and conversational skills, such as the ability to adapt language to the needs of present or nonpresent listeners.

There is considerable controversy about the level of proficiency in a second language needed to support reading in that language. Wong Fillmore and Valadez (1986) argue that second-language reading for English-language learners should not be introduced until a fairly high level of second-language proficiency has been achieved. However, Anderson and Roit (1996), Gersten (1996), and others argue that instruction focused on second-language reading comprehension can be helpful to learners at all levels of second-language oral proficiency, even for those with learning disabilities (Klingner and Vaughn, 1996), and in fact that support of second-language reading comprehension can generate gains in second-language oral skills (see also Elley, 1981).

In general, positive correlations have been found between English second-language oral proficiency and English second-language reading ability, particularly at higher grade levels, but not equally across all first-language groups (Devine, 1987; see Fitzgerald, 1995, for a review). The mixed findings may well reflect differences in oral language proficiency measures used across the various studies and in conditions for literacy acquisition. For example, older, already literate second-language learners acquiring English literacy through formal, foreign-language-type instruction may rely less on oral language as a route to English literacy than those acquiring their initial literacy skills in the second language.

Optimal Early Reading Instruction

Perhaps the most controversial area in reading research is the question of how best to teach initial reading—the whole-word method (Flesch, 1955), phonics/direct instruction methods, or whole-language methods (Chall, 1967, 1983; Adams, 1990).[1]

While one can cite research findings in support of the value of certain of these practices over others, only recently has anyone officially sanctioned a mixed method of teaching reading—embedding direct instruction in component processes into meaningful, communicative, literate activities—that many experienced and successful teachers are in fact implementing in their classrooms (Adams and Bruck, 1995; Purcell-Gates, 1996).

With regard to reading instruction in a second language, there is remarkably little directly relevant research. Clearly one of the major intellectual stimuli to bilingual education programs has been the belief that initial reading instruction in a language not yet mastered orally to some reasonable level is too great a cognitive challenge for most learners. Studies of outcomes of bilingual programs, however, do not typically distinguish students who arrive at school already reading in their first language from those who learn to read only at school. The evidence that better academic outcomes characterize immigrant children who have had 2 to 3 years of initial schooling (and presumably literacy instruction) in their native countries (Collier and Thomas, 1989; Skutnabb-Kangas, 1979) is consistent with the claim that children should first learn to read in a language they already speak. However, it is clear that many children first learn to read in a second language without serious negative consequences. These include children who successfully go through early-immersion,

---

[1]The whole-word method involves teaching reading by having children acquire a large repertoire of sight words, without providing direct instruction in the regularities of English orthography. The phonics method focuses on teaching and providing practice in the orthographic system, i.e., sound-letter relationships, the rules governing the interpretation of orthographic cues such as the silent 'e,' and the pronunciation of minor spelling patterns such as 'igh,' and 'ough.' The whole-language method emphasizes providing children with rich, authentic literacy experiences so they can discover the rules of English orthography themselves. Unlike the whole-word method, it does not involve teaching sight words.

two-way, and English as a second language (ESL)-based programs in North America, as well as those in formerly colonial countries that have maintained the official language as the medium of instruction, immigrant children in Israel, children whose parents opt for elite international schools, and many others (see Christian, 1996; Feitelson, 1988).

What we know about early literacy acquisition suggests it is more likely than not to be successful under a wide variety of circumstances, but is nonetheless impacted by a long list of risk factors, including lack of explicit instruction in the local orthography, absence of the sort of background knowledge and skills acquired in highly literate environments, and unfamiliarity with the words one is trying to read. Exposure to any one of these and other risk factors may have no impact on literacy achievement, though the coincidence of several may lead to a greater likelihood of failure. The high literacy achievement of Spanish-speaking children in English-medium Success for All schools (Slavin and Yampolsky, 1992) that feature carefully designed direct literacy instruction suggests that even children from low-literacy homes can learn to read in a second language if the risk associated with poor instruction is eliminated.

Reading as a Developmental Process

There are rather different tasks and skills involved in reading at various points in the acquisition of skilled reading: learning about print versus nonprint, typically accomplished in the preschool years; learning to recognize and write letters; learning to decode words, which involves synthesizing phonological from graphemic sequences; reading relatively simple texts fluently; reading for comprehension texts that include new information and unknown lexical items; reading strategically, for specific information or purposes such as relaxation; and reading critically, to examine and compare the claims and arguments of different authors. The essential idea here is that the nature of reading skill needs to be defined somewhat differently at different points in its development, and thus that acquisition of prior skills does not always predict continued growth in reading ability; there are several points in development where novel skills need to be acquired.

The implications of this view for second-language learners are potentially enormous, as the task of learning to read in a second language is presumably quite different at different stages of first-language reading skill. Direct studies of the nature of what can be transferred from first- to second-language reading need to take into account not only the level of first-language reading, but also the level and content of the second-language material being read, as well as the nature of the orthographic, linguistic, and rhetorical differences between the first and second languages.

Comprehension of Skilled Readers

Skilled readers are capable of reading with understanding in part because the component processes—letter recognition, word recognition, access to word meaning, syntactic parsing of the sentence—are fast and efficient (e.g., Adams, 1990). Those who have poor skills in word recognition can improve their comprehension by employing strategies such as reading the whole text for gist; self-monitoring for understanding; and using cues from titles, pictures, headings, and the like.

Explicit instruction in comprehension strategies such as prediction, summarization, and questioning—for example, the widely used "reciprocal teaching" (Palincsar and Brown, 1984) or Bereiter and Bird's (1985) think-aloud method—has been shown to be useful with poor first-language readers, and some evidence suggests it would also be useful with second-language readers who have comprehension difficulties (e.g., Barnett, 1989; Casanave, 1988; Cohen, 1990). Studies of the metacognitive strategies used by second-language readers of English reveal that such strategies are widely used (reviewed in Fitzgerald, 1995). The repertoire of those strategies includes some that may be specific to the second-language situation, such as using translation dictionaries or relying on information about cognates, but many are also typical of first-language readers as well, such as asking questions, predicting, and summarizing. However, some researchers have suggested that rather little attention is given to teaching or promoting comprehension strategies for English-language learners, even in the middle and later elementary grades when such instruction is important, because teachers tend to focus on word recognition and pronunciation (e.g., Gersten, 1996).

Skilled readers use syntactic information unconsciously to make the reading process more efficient, for example, by fixating on high-information items in the text (Rayner and Pollatsek, 1989). The fact that high-information items differ from language to language can lead to inefficient fixation patterns when reading in a second language (Bernhardt, 1987), thus perhaps disrupting the fluency that facilitates comprehension.

Skilled readers can tolerate a small proportion of unknown words in texts without disruption of comprehension and can even infer the meanings of those words from sufficiently rich contexts, but if the proportion of unknown words is too high, comprehension is disrupted. Word knowledge no doubt relates to reading comprehension both because encountering many unknown words slows processing and because lack of word knowledge indicates absence of the relevant background knowledge that is crucial in reading texts of any complexity. Familiarity with content promotes reading comprehension when reading in either a second or a first language (Carrell, 1987; Johnson, 1981; see Fitzgerald, 1995, for a review), though knowledge of relevant background information may be less reliably indexed by second- than first-language vocabulary.

Comprehension is also supported by familiarity with larger structural patterns present in texts. Knowing that paragraphs have topic sentences on which other sentences are meant to elaborate, for example, aids the reader in integrating information across sentences. These macrostructures are culturally determined. For example, the writings of Michener, Allende, and Oe display wide variation in notions of plot and temporal sequence, of how much orientation is needed, and of how much interpretation should be supplied. In general, passages organized in a familiar structure are easier to comprehend and recall for second-language readers than those with a novel rhetorical structure (see Fitzgerald, 1995, for a review).

Content Learning

Considerable progress has been made over the last two decades in understanding the nature and processes of the learning and acquisition of knowledge of specific content information. This research has, for the most part, not concerned itself with issues of language per se, nor has it been incorporated into discussions about English-language learners.

Because the problem for the English-language learner has been considered as almost entirely language based, much of the research has focused on language acquisition issues. But the learning of school subject matter and work skills involves building intricate networks of concept relations, structuring and restructuring understandings, connecting them to other understandings, and practicing multiple skills in multiple environments. Therefore, more complex questions might fruitfully be asked about the nature of second-language students' learning, knowledge, and understanding of complex subject matter domains.

Discussion of complex questions of subject matter learning for English-language learners needs to be grounded in some assumptions about learning in general. The remainder of this section describes three assumptions drawn from cognitive analyses about school subject matter learning for primary-language content learning. These assumptions provide the context for much of the current research on school learning and apply to most students and most subject matter domains. First, we assume that different subjects have different core structures or epistemologies, thus making different demands on the learner. Second, we assume that there are multiple forms or kinds of knowledge—for example, knowledge of facts and ideas, as well as knowledge of how to do something. Third, we assume that prior knowledge plays a significant role in learning, not only in terms of where to start, but also in terms of the actual meanings attached to new information. The discussion of these assumptions offers some examples and examines what a program of cognitive research that considered subject matter learning for English-language learners might look like.

Subject Matter Specificity

Although learning, knowledge, and understanding differ across subject matter, these differences are embedded in larger general similarities. For example, understanding and learning about earth science or social studies requires the general ability to read, to construct meaning, and to understand and follow oral discussion in the language of instruction. It also requires general capabilities of inferencing, placing examples into overarching constructs, and building causal chains.[2]

Knowledge varies both across and within subject matter areas: it varies across because subjects have different arrangements of facts, concepts, notations, and patterns of reasoning; it varies within because some academic subjects have elaborate and importantly constraining notational systems (for example, algebraic and graphic systems).

The fundamental differences among subject areas necessitate highly differentiated systems of complex knowledge for both students and their teachers. While it is clear that at some level of abstraction, generalities across subject areas do exist, we believe these generalities are not sufficient to leapfrog the middle ground of differentiated knowledge. Further, a better understanding of this middle ground can enhance our understanding of the nature of both primary-language content learning and content learning in a second language.

In light of these differences among the various subject areas, certain disciplines may lend themselves more easily than others to the transfer of knowledge across languages, depending on the structure of knowledge within the domain, but the particular domains to which this would apply are not readily apparent. Because sophisticated knowledge in a given domain not only uses the terminology of that domain, but also builds upon

---

[2]Between these bottom-up skills (Kintsch and van Dijk, 1978) and top-down schemas (Anderson and Pearson, 1984) lies a rather large domain of highly differentiated systems of knowledge, for which expertise also tends to be differentiated (Chi et al., 1982; Schwab, 1978; Stodolsky, 1988).

gradually developing concepts, learning such strands of content knowledge in one language and then shifting to another may be especially problematic.

Although there are substantial differences among subject matter areas, studies of English-language learners and their teachers seem to have ignored these distinctions, instead identifying a central problem facing these students as learning enough general language to enter English-only classrooms. We do not know what the advantages or complications are for English-language learners trying to learn the various disciplines themselves. However, we do suggest that it would be useful to learn how general language proficiencies interact with specific academic language proficiencies and with specific subject matter content.

Multiple Forms of Knowledge

Not only are there substantial differences among subject matter areas, but there are also different kinds of knowledge. One of the more common distinctions among types of knowledge is that between procedural knowledge, or knowledge of actions and skills, and declarative knowledge, or knowledge of concepts and principles (Chi and Ceci, 1987; Heibert, 1986; Lampert, 1986; Scribner, 1984). One task facing the student is to integrate these two types of knowledge.

Another distinction between types of knowledge is between knowledge of content and knowledge of that knowledge, referred to as metacognition. Brown (1980) discusses metacognition in terms of three features: knowing what you know and how well you know it, knowing what you need to know, and knowing the utility of active intervention. This self-awareness has been found to be a useful tool for learners across domains. Learners with such awareness are better able to organize the knowledge they have and identify the knowledge they need to acquire.

We do not have much information about the English-language learner with respect to multiple forms of knowledge. (See Chapter 7 for a review of studies that examine the effect of instruction in metacognitive skills on the subject matter learning of English-language learners.) However, issues of metacognition have been discussed for second-language learners in terms of the additive principle, which suggests these students have an advantage when learning new material.[3] The argument that metacognitive

---

[3]It is striking how little research has been carried out on the metacognitive capacities of bilinguals, given the robust findings concerning their metalinguistic superiority. Bilinguals' abstract metalinguistic understanding of the structure of language may facilitate their learning of new material (Bialystok and Hakuta, 1994; Cummins, 1991; Diaz, 1986; Hakuta and Diaz, 1985; Peal and Lambert, 1962).

abilities facilitate learning by primary-language content learners lends support to the claim of the additive principle. Note, however, that in considering metacognition, the assumed advantage for second-language learners when learning new material has been focused strictly on linguistic awareness; the findings do not generalize to utility for learning particular subject matter knowledge.

Prior Knowledge

The types and amount of knowledge available before encountering a new topic within a particular discipline affect how meaning is constructed. The knowledge structure can be thought of as nodes of information, such as concepts, that are linked to each other in particular ways depending on how and what information has been learned. Links between concepts can be acquired, reconstructed, or deconstructed, and particular learning outcomes are determined jointly by what was known before (the unique pattern of nodes and links) and the effects of instruction (additions to or rearrangements of that pattern).

The issue of prior knowledge can be considered one of depth, interconnectedness, and access. Depth of knowledge refers to the number of linked concepts a student has in a domain. In math, for example, students' depth of knowledge will influence their recognition of a problem, their sense of meaning associated with the problem, their ability to perform the appropriate mathematical operations, and their ability to recognize a reasonable answer. The extent to which concepts are interconnected reveals the coherence of a student's understanding of a particular domain. Finally, the existence of different kinds of knowledge poses a problem for both teaching and learning in that if the different types of knowledge are disconnected, they will be inert and unusable (Bereiter, 1984; Brown et al., 1983). A student may know what a long division problem is, but not know how to solve it. The development of deep, interconnected, generative knowledge instead of shallow, fragmented, inert knowledge needs to be a continuous process for both teachers and their students, with the interaction between the two forms of knowledge being explicitly taught.

Thus the depth, interconnectedness, and accessibility of prior knowledge all dramatically influence the processing of new information (Chi and Koeske, 1983; McKeown et al., 1992; Pearson et al., 1979). With respect to second-language learners, then, a number of questions arise. Under what conditions is content learning affected by the fact that a superordinate category and its instantiation (e.g., commutivity and addition) are learned both tacitly and explicitly in one language, but are then to be used as a principle in a more complex instantiation in another language (e.g., addition of algebraic polynomials)? How are "errors" that have a language base handled in a second language (e.g., in English, the confusion of "north" with "up" on a page versus in real space)? Naturally, the potential for interference in terms of access is also of concern—although this may be a vocabulary issue. A problem may arise if base examples are introduced at a young age in the child's first language (e.g., for social studies, notions of community, roles, freedom, and power) and are to be built upon in the second language at a later age (e.g., in learning about the French Revolution). Does this affect the second-language learner, and how?

At this point, we know next to nothing about how to answer these questions. We do not know, for example, whether (especially for the older new arrival) time should be taken to review existing knowledge that is available in the first language in a way that recontextualizes it in the second language, or whether the new knowledge (e.g., Algebra II) should simply be supported with back references to salient ideas known in the first language but now used in the second (e.g., Algebra I). The literature discussed here could be used to broaden the debate on content learning for English-language learners to address such issues.

IMPLICATIONS

Educational

Many of the findings regarding effective instruction and risk factors associated with reading for English-only students can be applied to English-language learners. An example is the benefit of a mixed method of teaching reading—embedding direct instruction of component processes into meaningful, communicative, literate activities. However, there are other important factors that must be taken into consideration in teaching English-language learners to read in English. For example, because there are rather different tasks and skills involved in reading at various points in the acquisition of skilled reading, the discussion of what can be transferred from first- to second-language reading needs to take into account not only the level of first-language reading, but also the level and content of the second-language material being read, as well as the nature of the orthographic, linguistic, and rhetorical differences between the first and second languages. Comprehension is supported by employing strategies such as reading the whole text for gist, self-monitoring for understanding, and using cues from titles, pictures, headings, and the like; by asking questions, predicting, and summarizing; by increasing word knowledge using translation dictionaries or relying on information about cognates; and by gaining familiarity with larger structural patterns present in texts.

Three assumptions provide the context for much of the current research on school learning and apply to most students and most subject matter domains: (1) different subjects have different core structures or epistemologies, thus making different demands on the learner; (2) there are multiple forms or kinds of knowledge—for example, knowledge of facts and ideas, as well as knowledge of how to do something; and (3) prior knowledge plays a significant role in learning in terms not only of where to start, but also of the actual meanings attached to new information. Although most of this research has not been conducted with English-language learners, we can reasonably assume until proven otherwise that it applies to these students and points to the importance of understanding their acquisition of content knowledge.

Research

Research is needed on language-literacy relationships. It is also needed on the nature of the relationship between first- and second-language literacy skill.

Research needs to investigate the optimal English literacy instruction for children of different ages, those with different native languages, those whose native language is not written, and those whose parents are not literate in English. Is there a single best way to teach all children to read, and if not, is there some way to identify child aptitudes so as to define optimal individualized instruction? What should be the role of writing in reading instruction, particularly for second-language learners? An important question to be addressed is whether literacy can be used as a route to language learning, and if so, under what circumstances and with what consequences.

There are four key research questions that address how those with limited English proficiency learn content. First, what are the effects of limited English proficiency on the acquisition of content knowledge at a fine-grained level? Specifically, what are the consequences of acquiring beginning-level content knowledge in one language and then switching languages for higher levels of the content domain? Second, what levels of English proficiency are prerequisite to the capacity to profit from content area instruction in English? Third, are there modifications to the language used by teachers that can make complex subject matters accessible even to second-language beginners? Fourth, how does the presence of a second language in the classroom affect the cognitive load for the content area teacher?

THE SOCIAL CONTEXT OF SCHOOL LEARNING:
KEY FINDINGS

Research based on the premise that schooling must be analyzed from social as well as cognitive perspectives has yielded a number of key findings:

- In classroom learning situations, negotiation occurs within at least two domains: the rules for how to talk in the classroom and the construction of actual content knowledge through talk. The implications for English-language learners are that negotiating these matters is much more difficult in a second language, and negotiated rules are likely to be heavily influenced by culture.
- English-language learners may be treated differently from mainstream students as a result of forces both within and outside of school that implicitly and explicitly promote and sustain the perspectives and institutions of the majority.
- While achievement motivation is an important factor in helping explain school success, it does not explain differences in success among language-minority groups or between immigrant and mainstream groups.
- The language and dialects spoken by children influence teacher perceptions of their academic ability, the students' learning opportunities, evaluations of their contributions to class, and the way they are grouped for instruction. The languages students speak also influence perceptions of their academic ability and their learning opportunities.
- Research on cooperative learning indicates that students of color and white students have a greater tendency to make cross-racial friendship choices after they have participated in interracial cooperative learning teams, and the academic achievement of students of color is increased when cooperative learning activities are used. Cooperative learning activities also increase student motivation and self-esteem and help students develop empathy.
- Curriculum interventions—multi-ethnic and -racial lessons and materials—have positive effects on the ethnic and racial attitudes of students.
- Like all students, English-language learners benefit from actions taken in the home to promote child academic achievement. Such activities can be classified as monitoring, communication, motivational, and protective. However, these actions may not be visible to school personnel, who thus assume parents are uninvolved in their children's learning.

4

The Social Context of School Learning

Whereas the previous chapter reviewed cognitive aspects of literacy and content learning, this chapter examines research related to a variety of social factors involved in school learning. It is clear that children may arrive at school ready to learn in a number of different ways. One way is to have high levels of language, emergent literacy, and world knowledge acquired at home or in preschool. Equally important, though, is readiness in the emotional, social, and motivational realms: the ability to adapt to the new constraints of the classroom, the social skills needed to participate effectively in classroom discourse, and the self-esteem and sense of agency required to work hard and learn intentionally. Moreover, other aspects of the social context, such as differential treatment of minority children, impact school learning.

FINDINGS

This section focusses on five areas: the social nature of knowledge acquisition, the issue of differential treatment of ethnic-minority students, cultural differences in the motivation to achieve, children's social and group relationships, and parental involvement in children's school learning.

The Social Nature of Knowledge Acquisition

Were we to focus only on issues examined in the previous two chapters, we would be ignoring a vital aspect of school learning: that most learning occurs in a social context in which individual actions and understandings are negotiated by the members of a group. We propose that in a classroom learning situation, negotiation occurs within at least two domains: the rules for how to talk in the classroom and the construction of actual content knowledge through talk. It is from the interpretation of these negotiations that students construct their own knowledge and understanding. However, it is typically the teacher who, either implicitly or explicitly, initiates negotiation.

Conversational Rules

The process of negotiating the way classroom participants will talk about subject matter is assumed to influence an individual's academic performance. There are obvious implications for second-language education, in part because negotiating engagement in conversation is much more difficult in a second language and in part because the negotiated rules are likely to be heavily influenced by culture. Based on observations of children both at home (Philips, 1983; Heath, 1983) and at school (Gee, 1988a, 1988b; Michaels, 1991; Au and Mason, 1981; Au, 1980; Boggs, 1985), researchers conclude that there is cultural mismatch in the negotiation of talk that limits full participation in educational interactions for second-language learners.

Phillips (1983) found that Native American students' verbal interactions were much more extensive in classrooms whose participant structures were similar to those used routinely in their homes and communities. Various studies have investigated efforts to incorporate into classrooms features of learning and talking that are characteristic of the homes and communities of English-language learners. Perhaps the most well-known such effort to make classroom instruction culturally responsive is the Kamehameha Early Education Program (Au and Mason, 1981), which incorporated the talk story format, a native Hawaiian discourse pattern, into literacy instruction, with positive results.

Negotiating Knowledge

In addition to negotiation of the rules for classroom talk, social practices for talking about a particular subject matter are also negotiated by the participants. Researchers have contributed to our understanding of the language and social practices in classrooms and the role of these patterns in the construction of knowledge (*Linguistics and Education*, 1994; Goldenberg and Gallimore, 1991; Rueda et al., 1992; Saunders et al., 1992; Patthey-Chavez and Goldenberg, 1995; Dalton and Sison, 1995). For example, in her ethnographic study of journal sharing in nine different bilingual classrooms, Gutierrez (1992, 1994) found that teachers shared one of three "scripts" or pedagogical views of writing. Based on Gutierrez's 1992 descriptions, only one of these scripts provided enriched contexts for literacy learning in line with the tenets of sociocultural theory, that is, "contexts that give students both assistance and the occasions to use and write elaborated and meaningful discourse" (p. 259).

Differential Treatment

While cultural mismatch is one explanation for the relatively poor academic performance of English-language learners, another avenue of research, known as differential treatment studies, starts from the assumption that some language-minority children may not be socialized toward academic achievement. This literature has contributed to the view that language-minority students, along with other ethnic-minority students, are treated differently from mainstream students as a result of forces both within and outside of school that implicitly and explicitly promote and sustain the perspectives and institutions of the majority. Ogbu, a primary contributor to this view (Ogbu, 1978; Ogbu and Matute-Bianchi, 1986), has focused on how societal forces have contributed to socialization and acculturation patterns that ultimately influence minority students' academic achievement. Other researchers (Moll and Diaz, 1987; Gibson, 1988; Suarez-Orozco and Suarez-Orozco, 1995; Tuan, 1995; Harklau, 1994) have concentrated on schools and classrooms when investigating the interaction among cultural, societal, and school influences on student achievement. The latter studies have shown how schools engage in a number of practices that favor the status quo by enabling middle- and upper-class English-speaking students to progress through an educational pipeline that is often inaccessible to low-income ethnic-minority students, including those who are limited-English-proficient.

Cultural Differences in Achievement Motivation

Achievement motivation—the set of beliefs children hold about how and why to do well in school—is implicated in the relatively poor perfor-

mance of language-minority children. The notion that achievement motivation may vary culturally has been supported by cross-national studies
(e.g., Stevenson et al., 1990; Stevenson et al., 1986) showing that Asian
children are more likely to believe high achievement is the result of effort,
whereas American children focus more on innate ability. In the United
States, however, these ethnic differences are eliminated or even reversed:
second-generation Korean American children have been found to attribute
success to ability more than do European American children (Choi et al.,
1994), and high achievers across a variety of ethnic groups (African
American, Latino, Indochinese American, and European American), all
low-income, attribute their success to their high innate ability (Bempechat
et al., 1996).

One consequence of assimilation is often a lowering of academic
goals and achievement, perhaps because of incorporation into a caste-like
minority status or peer stigmatization of high achievement (Ogbu, 1995).
It may be that some Asian immigrants are less susceptible to the negative
consequences of assimilation because, as voluntary immigrants, they place
their faith in schools as agents of improvement (DeVos, 1978).

Children's Social and Group Relationships

Dialects and languages spoken by students influence teacher perceptions of the students' academic ability, their learning opportunities, evaluations of their contributions to class, and the way they are grouped for
instruction (Harrison, cited in Garcia, 1993; Ryan and Carranza, 1977).
Language can be the basis as well for categorization and the formation of
ingroups and outgroups, especially within an institutional context in which
the languages spoken have unequal status. Languages are often symbols
of group boundaries and are therefore the sources of intergroup conflicts
and tensions (Giles, 1977; Issacs, 1992).

Two-way bilingual programs, in which students from two different
language groups learn both languages, may provide an effective way of
reducing group differences and constructing a single group identity (Lambert and Cazabon, 1994). Cooperative learning has also been found to
improve intergroup relations. In his review of 19 studies of the effects of
cooperative learning methods, Slavin (1985) found that 16 showed positive effects on interracial friendships. In a more recent review, Slavin
(1995) also describes the positive effects of cooperative groups on cross-
racial friendships, racial attitudes, and behavior.

Cohen and Roper (1972) caution, however, that equal status among
groups in interracial and interethnic situations must be constructed by
teachers, rather than assumed. In a series of perceptive and carefully

designed studies that span two decades, Cohen and colleagues (Cohen, 1984a, 1984b; Cohen and Roper, 1972; Cohen and Lotan, 1995) have consistently found that contact among different groups without deliberate interventions to increase equal status and positive interactions will increase rather than reduce intergroup tensions. Cohen (1994) has developed practical guidelines and strategies that can be used by teachers and other practitioners to create equal status within racially, culturally, and linguistically diverse classrooms.

Research indicates that curriculum interventions such as multiethnic curricular materials, plays, folk dances, music, and role playing can also have positive effects on the ethnic and racial attitudes of students (Gimmestad and DeChiara, 1982; McGregor, 1993).

Parental Involvement in Children's School Learning

When parents establish partnerships with their children's schools, they extend school learning effectively into the home and reinforce academic values outside school (Henderson, 1987; Dornbusch and Ritter, 1988). Positive effects of such partnerships have been found with both low- and middle-income populations, as well as populations of different racial/ethnic groups (Comer, 1986; Delgado-Gaitan, 1990; Epstein and Dauber, 1991; Dauber and Epstein, 1993; Hidalgo et al., 1995; Robledo Montecel, 1993). Evidence suggests that immigrant and language-minority children benefit from actions taken in the home to promote child academic achievement (Hidalgo et al., 1995; Diaz-Soto, 1988). However, teachers' notions of desirable parental involvement (coming to conferences, responding to notes, and participating in the classroom) may be foreign to immigrant parents (Allexsaht-Snider, 1992; Matsuda, 1989). Parent centers designed to promote the exchange of information regarding teacher expectations for parental involvement (Johnson, 1993, 1994; Rubio, 1995), two-generation literacy programs (McCollum, 1993), parent training seminars (Smith, 1993), and the Teachers Involve Parents in Schoolwork program (Epstein et al., 1995) have all been demonstrated to help align parental involvement with teacher expectations.

IMPLICATIONS

Educational

Because cultural mismatch in conversational patterns makes access to full participation in classroom interactions more difficult for the speakers of less-valued discourse forms, teachers need to be aware that full participation in these interactions will be challenging for English-language learners. Thus they might explore ways of more fully engaging culturally diverse students. Schools must also take care not to engage in practices that favor the status quo by enabling middle- and upper-class English-speaking students to progress through an educational pipeline that is often inaccessible to low-income ethnic-minority students, including those who are limited-English-proficient. Moreover, studies incorporating into the classroom features of learning and talking that are characteristic of the homes and communities of English-language learners have shown positive results.

Two-way bilingual programs, in which students from two different language groups learn both languages, may provide an effective way of reducing group differences and improving intergroup relations. Cooperative learning has also been found to improve intergroup relations. However, equal status between groups in interracial and interethnic situations must be constructed by teachers rather than assumed, since contact among different groups without deliberate interventions to increase equal status and positive interactions will increase rather than reduce intergroup tensions. Curriculum interventions such as multiethnic curricular materials, plays, folk dances, music, and role playing can also have positive effects on the ethnic and racial attitudes of students.

Evidence suggests that immigrant and language-minority children benefit from actions taken in the home to promote child academic achievement. Parent centers designed to promote the exchange of information regarding teacher expectations for parental involvement, two-generation literacy programs, parent training seminars, and the Teachers Involve Parents in Schoolwork program have all been demonstrated to help align parental involvement with teacher expectations.

Research

There are two important questions for research regarding status differences among various languages. First, what are the consequences of such differences for children's intergroup and interpersonal relations? Second, how do teachers' perceptions of the status of children's languages influence their interactions with, expectations of, and behavior toward the children?

Additional research is also needed to examine what innovative classroom organizations and interventions, such as curriculum content, can influence children's views of themselves and of members of other ethnic groups, promoting cross-ethnic friendships and positive regard.

Research is needed as well to examine the nature of socialization practices in the homes of English-language learners with regard to both content (e.g., exposure to literacy, opportunities for participation in substantive conversations) and socialization in ways of learning (e.g., through observation versus participation, in a relationship of collaboration versus respectful distance from the expert).

In addition, research needs to address the alignment between home and school. For example, does excellent instruction take into account home-school mismatches or simply teach children the school discourse effectively? Are there classroom structures and practices that are particularly familiar to English-language learners and thus promote their learning by minimizing home-school mismatches? Are there procedures for inducting English-language learners into novel classroom and instructional interactions that can promote their learning both of English and of subject matter?

STUDENT ASSESSMENT:
KEY FINDINGS

From the literature on student assessment, the following key findings can be drawn:

- Several uses of assessment are unique to English-language learners and bilingual children. They include identification of children whose English proficiency is limited, determination of eligibility for placement in specific language programs, and monitoring of progress in and readiness to exit from special language service programs.
- English-language learners are assessed for purposes that extend beyond determination of their language needs, including placement in categorically funded education programs such as Title I, placement in remedial or advanced classwork, monitoring of achievement in compliance with district- and/or state-level programs, and certification for high school graduation and determination of academic mastery at graduation.
- It is essential that any assessment impacting children's education strive to meet standards of validity (whether inferences drawn are appropriate to the purposes of the assessment) and reliability (whether assessment outcomes are accurate in light of variations due to factors irrelevant to what the assessment was intended to measure).
- States and local districts use a variety of methods to determine which students need to be placed in special language-related programs and monitor students' progress in those programs. Administration of language proficiency tests is the most common method. Achievement tests in English are also frequently used.
- Regardless of the modality of testing, many existing English-language proficiency instruments emphasize measurement of a limited range of grammatical and structural skills.
- States use a variety of procedures to assess student academic performance, including performance-based assessments and standardized achievement tests, and states are in various stages of incorporating English-language learners into these assessments.
- To a large extent, the field lacks instruments appropriate for assessing very young English-language learners, as well as English-language learners with disabilities.
- The standards-based reform movement has major implications for the assessment of English-language learners.

5

Student Assessment

This chapter addresses the issue of assessing the language proficiency and subject matter knowledge and skills of English-language learners.[1] Assessment plays a central role in the education of English-language learners and bilingual children. Teachers generally use assessments to monitor language development in students' first or second language and track the quality of their day-to-day subject matter learning. In addition, "high stakes" assessments are used to place students in special programs and to provide information for accountability and policy analysis purposes.

Garcia and Pearson (1994:343-349) examine assessment for culturally diverse learners across a wide range of subject matters and test types. They highlight potential validity and reliability problems for English-language learners that result from the "mainstream bias" of formal testing, including a norming bias (small numbers of particular minorities included in probability samples, increasing the likelihood that minority group samples are unrepresentative), content bias (test content and procedures

---

[1]The standards for assessing reading and writing developed by the International Reading Association and the National Committee of Teachers of English, as well as those developed by Teachers of English to Speakers of Other Languages for assessing English proficiency, are consistent with and supportive of the model of assessment emerging from the review in this chapter.

reflecting the dominant culture's standards of language function and shared knowledge and behavior), and linguistic and cultural biases (factors that adversely affect the formal test performance of students from diverse linguistic and cultural backgrounds, including timed testing, difficulty with English vocabulary, and the near impossibility of determining what bilingual students know in their two languages).

The ensuing discussion of assessment as applied to English-language learners and bilingual children inherently involves questions about the validity and reliability of assessments and their appropriateness for these children. It is also important to note that assessment practices have social and educational consequences that should be considered in an ongoing program of validity research (Messick, 1988).

FINDINGS

This section begins with two subsections that review issues involved in assessing language proficiency and those associated with the assessment of subject matter knowledge. The next two subsections examine uses of assessment that are unique to and those that extend beyond English-language learners. Issues associated with assessing special populations are then explored. The section ends with a discussion of standards-based reform and its implications for the design and conduct of student assessments.

Issues in Assessing Language Proficiency

In assessing the language proficiency of English-language learners, both discrete language skills (e.g., vocabulary and grammar) and more authentic and holistic uses of language should be assessed. The assessment of discrete language skills is a legitimate endeavor because each of these components is systemically related to authentic use of language (McLaughlin, 1984). However, many researchers in this area (Rivera, 1984; Wong Fillmore, 1982; Valdez Pierce and O'Malley, 1992) recommend assessment procedures that reflect tasks typical of classroom or real-life settings, such as oral interviews, story retellings, simulations, directed dialogues, incomplete story/topic prompts, picture cues, teacher observation checklists, student self-evaluations, and portfolios. Authentic assessments are both more difficult to administer and less objectively scored than traditional assessments, but they do reflect the important view that language proficiency is multifaceted and varies according to the task demands and content area domain (see Chapter 2).

Most measures used to assess English proficiency have measured decontextualized skills and set fairly low standards for language proficiency. Ultimately, English-language learners should be held to high standards for both English language and literacy, and should transition from being assessed with special measures of their increasing command of English to full participation in regularly administered assessments of English-language arts.

Issues in Assessing Subject Matter Knowledge

In this section, we examine the difficulties involved in incorporating English-language learners and bilingual children into subject matter assessments intended for their English-proficient peers.

As noted in the *Standards for Educational and Psychological Tests,* every assessment is an assessment of language (American Educational Research Association, American Psychological Association, and National Council on Measurement in Education, 1985). This is even more so given the advent of performance assessments requiring extensive comprehension and production of language. Given that the English-language proficiency levels of students affects their performance on subject area assessments administered in English (Garcia, 1991; Alderman, 1981) and that recently developed assessments require high levels of English proficiency, assessments and assessment procedures appropriate for English-language learners are needed. One strategy under active investigation is the use of native-language assessments. Approximately 75 percent of English-language learners come from Spanish-language backgrounds. For some of these students, it is realistic to develop native-language assessments. However, one must keep in mind the difficulties involved in developing native-language assessments that are equivalent to the English versions. Such difficulties include problems of regional and dialect differences, nonequivalence of vocabulary difficulty between two languages, problems of incomplete language development and lack of literacy development in students' primary languages, and the extreme difficulty of defining a "bilingual" equating sample (each new definition of a bilingual sample requires statistical equivalence among groups). Minimally, back translation should be done to determine equivalent meaning, and ideally, psychometric validation should be undertaken as well, such as validating the translated version with empirical evidence using item response theory (Hambleton and Kanjee, 1994).

Another strategy to make assessments both comprehensible and conceptually appropriate for English-language learners might entail decreasing the English-language load through actual modification of the items or instructions. This would not be a straightforward task, however. While some experts recommend reducing nonessential details and simplifying grammatical structures (Short, 1991), others claim that simplifying the surface linguistic features will not necessarily make the text easier to understand (Saville-Troike, 1991). When Abedi et al. (1995) reduced the linguistic complexity of National Assessment of Educational Progress mathematics test items in English, they reported only a modest and statistically unreliable effect in favor of the modified items for students at lower levels of English proficiency.

Other strategies for incorporating English-language learners into assessments include extra time, small-group administration, flexible scheduling, reading of directions aloud, use of dictionaries, and administration of the assessment by a person familiar with the children's primary language and culture (Rivera, 1995). Additional possibilities include making test instructions more explicit and allowing English-language learners to display their knowledge using alternative forms of representation (e.g., showing math operations on numbers and knowledge of graphing in problem solving). However, almost no research has been conducted to determine the effectiveness of these techniques.

Another issue in assessment of subject matter knowledge for English-language learners is the errors that result from inaccurate and inconsistent scoring of open-ended or performance-based measures. There is evidence that scorers may pay attention to linguistic features of performance unrelated to the content of the assessment. Thus, scorers may inaccurately assign low scores for performance in which English expression (either oral or written) is weak even though understanding or mastery of skills is high. This obviously confounds the accuracy of the score enormously.[2] Absent training, different scorers probably will rate the same student work very differently.

Some states also provide guidance to scorers on evaluating the work of English-language learners. Hafner (1995) reports that 10 percent of states give special training on evaluating the work of English-language

---

[2]Interestingly, Lindholm (1994) found highly significant and positive correlations between standardized scores of Spanish reading achievement and teacher-rated reading rubric scores, as well as between the standardized reading scores and students' ratings of their reading competence, for native English-speaking and native Spanish-speaking students enrolled in a bilingual immersion program.

learners, and 10 percent give directions in their manuals. Some training entails the development of scoring rubrics and procedures for constructed response items that are sensitive to the language and cultural characteristics of English-language learners. The Council of Chief State School Officers recently developed a scorer's training manual (Wong Fillmore and Lara, 1996) for use by states and local education agencies as an aid in the scoring of English-language learners' answers to open-ended mathematics questions. This manual will be piloted in collaboration with the National Center for Education Statistics and the Educational Testing Service, using the work of English-language learners who participated in the 1996 National Assessment of Educational Progress math assessment, to see how well it prepares scorers to assess the work of those students accurately.

Assessment Purposes Unique to English-Language Learners

Assessment purposes unique to English-language learners are focused on determining when these students should be placed in and exited from special language services such as English as a second language and bilingual education programs. There is a great deal of variability across school districts in the way assessments are used for these purposes. This variability exists because many states, while providing guidance to districts on assessment procedures, allow them considerable flexibility in choosing assessment methods, assessment instruments (usually from a menu of state-approved instruments), and cutoff scores for eligibility and classification for those instruments (August and Lara, 1996).[3]

---

[3]Of the 25 states that have assessment requirements for determining which language-minority students are of limited English proficiency, 22 specify English proficiency tests. Of these 22 states, 8 also specify achievement tests, and 3 specify English proficiency tests and below-average performance based on grades or classwork. When assessment is used for program placement, similar procedures are used. In the other states, it is up to individual districts to set these policies. In some states, native-language proficiency assessments are required (Arizona, Hawaii, Utah, California, Texas, New Jersey) or recommended. The only information regarding methods for reclassifying students from language assistance programs (Cheung and Soloman, 1991) indicates that language tests are the most frequently used method (required in 36 percent of states, recommended in 30 percent), followed by content area tests (required in 34 percent of states, recommended in 11 percent). Other methods recommended for determining program exit include observations and interviews. About one-third of states reported having no state requirement regarding exit criteria.

Assessment Purposes That Extend
Beyond English Language Learners

The assessment policies discussed in this section are related to determining eligibility for federal assistance and monitoring student progress at the state and district levels.

Title I

Specific attention is given to Title I, which is by far the largest federal program serving English-language learners. Changes in the Title I legislation provide for the participation of all students, including English-language learners, in assessments to determine whether they are meeting performance standards, and for reasonable adaptations of these assessments to this end. According to the law, English-language learners are to be included in assessments to the extent practicable, in the language and form most likely to yield accurate and reliable information on what they know and can do, including their mastery of skills in target subject matter areas, not just English. The law now further requires that each state plan identify the languages other than English that are present in the participating student population and indicate the languages for which yearly student assessments are not available and are needed. States are required to make every effort to develop such assessments and may request assistance from the U.S. Department of Education if linguistically accessible assessment measures are needed (see August et al., 1995).

Assessment is particularly important for purposes of selecting students eligible for services in Title I targeted assistance programs (as opposed to Title I school-wide programs), whereby Title I services are made available to a subset of the students "on the basis of multiple, educationally related, objective criteria established by the local educational agency and supplemented by the school" (Section 1115). The current policy guidance provided by the U.S. Department of Education does not elaborate on how equitable selection might be accomplished for English-language learners, and leaves it up to local districts to select those eligible students "most in need of special services." In the absence of test modifications, including assessments conducted in the native language, as well as methods for determining how English-language learners compare with other students on educational needs, a large proportion of English-language learners may not be served through Title I.

State, District, and Classroom Assessments

States are in various stages of incorporating English-language learners into performance-based assessments and standardized achievement tests, measures they use to monitor student performance (August and Lara, 1996; Rivera, 1995). August and Lara (1996) found that only 5 states require English-language learners to take state-wide assessments required of other students;[4] 36 states exempt English-language learners from such assessments, although 22 of those states require these students to take the assessments after a given period of time (usually 1-3 years). Some states base their assessment decision on the proficiency level of their English-language learners; of these, a few leave it up to local districts to determine which students have enough English proficiency to participate in the state-wide assessments. Finally, some states use multiple criteria to excuse students from state-wide assessments, including number of years in English-speaking classrooms, language proficiency scores, school achievement, and teacher judgment.

States use a variety of approaches to assess students that have been exempted from the state-wide assessments. Hafner (1995) reports that 55 percent of states allow modifications in the administration of at least one of their assessments to incorporate English-language learners. The most common modifications are extra time (20 states), small-group administration (18 states), flexible scheduling (16 states), simplification of directions (14 states), use of dictionaries (13 states), and reading of questions aloud in English (12 states). Other accommodations include assessments in languages other than English, availability of both English and non-English versions of the same assessment items, division of assessments into shorter parts, and administration of the assessment by a person familiar with the children's primary language and culture (Rivera, 1995).

Clearly, classroom teachers also assess students to determine how well they are grasping coursework and to inform instructional practice (see Chapter 7). Innovations at the classroom level include an assessment process that is multiple-referenced. That is, it incorporates information about the students in a variety of contexts obtained from a variety of sources through a variety of procedures (Genesee and Hamayan, 1994). Navarette et al. (1990) describe innovative assessment procedures that include unstructured techniques (e.g., writing samples, homework, logs, games, debates, story telling) and structured techniques (e.g., criterion-

---

[4]In 3 of these states, however, English-language learners may be exempted under certain conditions.

referenced tests, cloze tests, structured interviews), as well as portfolios that include both of these techniques. In addition, students are assessed in their native language to better determine their academic achievement and ensure appropriate coursework (Genesee and Hamayan, 1994). Information on student background characteristics, such as literacy in the home, parents' educational backgrounds, and previous educational experiences, is collected and provides essential information that helps put assessment results in context.

Issues in Assessing Special Populations

Very Young Second-Language Learners

The assessment of young children's development in meaningful ways is already surrounded by a great deal of controversy and concern among the preschool education community because of the dearth of valid and reliable instruments for measuring all aspects of child development (Meisels, 1994). For these reasons, McLaughlin et al. (1995) recommend what they call "instructionally embedded assessment," in which teachers make a plan about what, when, and how to assess a child; collect information from a variety of sources, including observations, prompted responses, classroom products, and conversations with family members; develop a portfolio; write narrative summaries; meet with family and staff; and finally, use the information to inform curriculum development. And this is a recursive process that begins again once it has been completed for any individual child. An assessment system of this sort is, of course, extremely time-consuming and necessitates reform in several areas, including use of time, professional staff development, accountability, and relationships with parents. It may, however, be the only meaningful way teachers can assess very young second-language learners.

Children with Disabilities

The field still lacks instruments appropriate for assessing English-language learners with disabilities. A practical strategy may be to train assessment personnel in appropriate procedures for this population, including acceptable modifications or alternatives, rather than awaiting the development of norm-referenced instruments appropriate for English-language learners.

The literature does identify several promising practices for assessing English-language learners with disabilities that may be useful as well for inclusion of all English-language learners in local and state assessments. Durán (1989) recommends the use of dynamic assessment (e.g., Feuerstein's [1979] Learning Potential Assessment Device), which involves a test-train-test cycle during which a student's response to a criterion problem is evaluated, feedback is given to help improve performance, and the student is reassessed. Lewis (1991) recommends use of the Kaufman Assessment Battery for Children (KABC) because it separates the mental processing scores from the achievement scores, and includes a training component to ensure that the student understands the task. He suggests that this approach accommodates different cognitive processing styles, an advantage in assessing diverse cultural groups. Further, he claims that Feuerstein's dynamic assessment approach and the KABC are more advantageous than instruments like the Weschler Intelligence Scales for Children-Revised (WISC-R) because they deemphasize factual information and learned content and focus instead on problem-solving tasks.

Because of the myriad of factors that must be considered in distinguishing linguistic and cultural differences from disabilities, ecological models of assessment are recommended so that learning problems will be examined in light of contextual variables affecting the teaching-learning process, including the interaction of teachers, students, curriculum, instructional variables, and so forth. Assessors must consider the student's native- and English-language skills, select appropriate measures for assessing skills across languages, and interpret outcomes considering factors such as the student's age and cultural and experiential background (Cloud, 1991).

Standards-Based Reform

The standards-based reform movement has major implications for English-language learners, especially in the area of assessment. Both Goals 2000 and the Improving America's Schools Act state explicitly that all students, including English-language-learners, are expected to attain high standards. For example, program accountability provisions in both Title I and Title VII are framed around the need to demonstrate that students in these programs are meeting state and local performance standards for all students. The demonstration of results has been a particularly complex issue for English-language learners because of the unavailability of assessments suited to their needs, as discussed previously.

Issues of validity and reliability in assessing the subject matter knowledge and skills of English-language learners were discussed earlier in this chapter. Another assessment issue related to standards-based reform is how to define adequate yearly progress for English-language learners. The Title I law, for example, requires that adequate yearly progress be defined in a manner that ". . . is sufficient to achieve the goal of all children served under [this part] in meeting the State's proficient and advanced levels of performance, particularly economically disadvantaged and LEP students." Yearly progress as defined by the law pertains to the progress of districts and schools, measured by the aggregation of individual student scores on assessments aligned with performance standards. According to the law, the same high performance standards that are established for all students are the ultimate goal for English-language learners as well.

On average, however, English-language learners (especially those with limited prior schooling) may take more time to meet these standards. Therefore, additional benchmarks might be developed for assessing the progress of these students toward meeting the standards. Moreover, because English-language learners are acquiring English-language skills and knowledge already possessed by students who arrive in school speaking English, additional content and performance standards in English-language arts may be appropriate. Recently, the Teachers of English to Speakers of Other Languages professional association has developed model content standards to guide the instruction and assessment of English skills and knowledge for such students (Teachers of English to Speakers of Other Languages, Inc., 1997).

Another issue related to adequate yearly progress has to do with districts' obligation to determine whether schools served by Title I funds are progressing sufficiently toward enabling all children to meet the state's student performance standards. According to the law, adequate progress is defined as that which results in continuous and substantial yearly improvement of each district and school, sufficient to achieve the goal of having all children—particularly economically disadvantaged students and English-language learners—meet the state's proficient and advanced levels of performance. To determine whether English-language learners are meeting these standards, assessment results must be disaggregated by English proficiency status. Some states, such as Florida, Hawaii, Louisiana, Maine, Ohio, and Washington, do this already (August and Lara, 1996). However, research is needed to determine how best to accomplish this goal in statistically sound ways, especially in light of alternative assessment procedures used with English-language learners.

Because of the difficulties in assessing English-language learners, it may be important to assess their access to necessary resources and conditions, such as adequate and appropriate instruction. However, defining and assessing these conditions is a very difficult task. Although there has been substantial work in defining some conditions, such as content coverage and time on task for mainstream students (Carroll, 1958; Leinhardt, 1978), the research base for defining the most important and effective resources and conditions for English-language learners is very weak (see Chapter 7). Yet many English-language learners do find themselves in poor schools with few resources. A good start would be to define and assess essential resources (e.g., textbooks, course offerings, accessibility of information) while continuing research into other aspects of school life, such as effective school-wide and classroom attributes that result in students' social and academic success. In terms of enhancing opportunities to learn for English-language learners, another strategy would be to encourage the development and evaluation of methods to help school staff monitor progress in improving schooling through systematic attempts to compare their school's performance against certain quality indicators.[5] This notion is further elaborated in Chapter 7.

IMPLICATIONS

Educational

To best inform instructional practice, an assessment process is recommended that incorporates information about students in a variety of contexts (i.e., home and school) obtained from a variety of sources (i.e., special language teachers and classroom teachers) through a variety of procedures (i.e., criterion-referenced tests, classroom observations, and portfolios).

To assess English-language proficiency, both discrete language skills (e.g., vocabulary and grammar) and more authentic and holistic uses of language should be assessed. Because English-language learners are acquiring English-language skills and knowledge already possessed by students who arrive in school speaking English, additional content and performance standards in English-language arts may be appropriate. Ultimately, English-language learners should be held to high standards for both English language and literacy, and should transition from being assessed with special measures of their increasing command of English to

---

[5]California, for example, has a Program Quality Review System that relies on peer review. Additional benchmarks could include school-wide and classroom factors that are known to improve the performance of English-language learners.

full participation in regularly administered assessments of English-language arts.

Strategies under active investigation for incorporating English-language learners into assessments of subject-matter knowledge include the use of native-language assessments. Other strategies for making assessments both comprehensible and conceptually appropriate for English-language learners entail a decrease in the English-language load of the assessment through actual modification of the items or instructions, extra time, small-group administration, flexible scheduling, reading of directions aloud, use of dictionaries, and administration of the assessment by a person familiar with the children's primary language and culture. However, additional research is needed to determine the psychometric soundness of these techniques. Finally, because of inaccurate and inconsistent scoring of open-ended or performance-based measures of English-language learner subject matter knowledge, training is needed so that such scoring is reliable.

Because of the difficulties in assessing English-language learners, it may be important to assess their access to necessary resources and conditions, such as adequate and appropriate instruction. However, defining and assessing these conditions is a very difficult task. In terms of enhancing opportunities to learn for English-language learners, another strategy would be to encourage the development and evaluation of methods to help school staff monitor progress in improving schooling through systematic attempts to compare their school's performance against certain quality indicators.

Research

Research is needed to improve native-language and English-language proficiency assessments so they are consistent with research findings on first- and second-language acquisition and literacy development.

Research is also needed to determine the levels of proficiency in different aspects of English required for English-language learners to participate in English-only instruction. Along the same lines, there is a need to develop guidelines for determining when English-language learners are ready to take the same assessments as their English-proficient peers, and when versions of an assessment other than the "standard" English version should be administered. There is a need as well to develop psychometrically sound and practical assessments and assessment procedures that incorporate English-language learners into district and state assessment systems. In addition, research is needed to improve inaccurate and inconsistent scoring of open-ended or performance-based measures of the work of English-language learners.

The field still lacks an array of instruments appropriate for assessing young English-language learners and those with disabilities. Several strategies are reviewed in this chapter, but should be evaluated to determine whether they are psychometrically sound.

Finally, to incorporate English-language learners into standards-based reform, research is needed in the following areas: (1) whether it is possible to establish common standard benchmarks for subject matter knowledge and English proficiency for English-language learners within a valid theoretical framework, what those benchmarks might be, and how the benchmarks for English proficiency might be related to performance standards for English-language arts; (2) how it can be determined whether, in the context of school and district outcomes, English-language learners are making progress toward meeting proficient and advanced levels of performance; and (3) how opportunities to learn can be evaluated.

PROGRAM EVALUATION:
KEY FINDINGS

The following key findings can be drawn from the literature on program evaluation:

- The major national-level program evaluations suffer from design limitations; lack of documentation of study objectives, conceptual details, and procedures followed; poorly articulated goals; lack of fit between goals and research design; and excessive use of elaborate statistical designs to overcome shortcomings in research designs.
- In general, more has been learned from reviews of smaller-scale evaluations, although these, too, have suffered from methodological limitations.
- It is difficult to synthesize the program evaluations of bilingual education because of the extreme politicization of the process. Most consumers of research are not researchers who want to know the truth, but advocates who are convinced of the absolute correctness of their positions.
- The beneficial effects of native-language instruction are clearly evident in programs that are labeled "bilingual education," but they also appear in some programs that are labeled "immersion." There appear to be benefits of programs that are labeled "structured immersion," although a quantitative analysis of such programs is not yet available.
- There is little value in conducting evaluations to determine which type of program is best. The key issue is not finding a program that works for all children and all localities, but rather finding a set of program components that works for the children in the community of interest, given that community's goals, demographics, and resources.

6

Program Evaluation

Of the types of programs for English-language learners reviewed in Chapter 1, the most commonly studied are those that use the native language for some limited period of time for core academics (e.g., transitional bilingual education programs) and those that do not use the native language in any regular or systematic way (i.e., English as a second language [ESL] and its variants, such as structured immersion and content-based ESL, as well as "submersion programs"). During the 1970s and 1980s, the federal government and advocates were keenly interested in determining which of these two models is more effective. Program evaluations were intended to provide a definitive answer to this question. This chapter examines what we know from program evaluations conducted to date. Chapter 7 reviews studies of school and classroom effectiveness.

FINDINGS

This section begins by reviewing national-level evaluations of programs for English-language learners and then examines reviews of smaller-scale program evaluations. This is followed by a discussion of the politicization of program evaluation. The final subsection addresses the future course of program evaluation, presenting five lessons learned that can lead to better, more useful evaluations.

National Evaluations

There have been three large-scale national evaluations of programs for English-language learners: the American Institutes for Research evaluation of programs, referred to as the AIR study (Dannoff, 1978); the National Longitudinal Evaluation of the Effectiveness of Services for Language Minority Limited English Proficient Students, referred to as the Longitudinal Study (Development Associates, 1984; Burkheimer et al., 1989); and the Longitudinal Study of Immersion and Dual Language Instructional Programs for Language Minority Children, referred to as the Immersion Study (Ramirez et al., 1991). This section summarizes these three studies, as well as the findings of a National Research Council report (Meyer and Fienberg, 1992) that reviews two of the three.

The AIR Study

The AIR study compared students enrolled in Title VII Spanish/English bilingual programs and comparable students (in terms of ethnicity, socioeconomic status, and grade level) not enrolled in such programs. For the study, 8,200 students were measured twice during the school year on English oral comprehension and reading, math, and Spanish oral comprehension and reading. Generally, the results from this study showed that students in bilingual education programs did not gain more in academic achievement than students not in such programs. However, the study was the subject of a great deal of criticism, the major criticism questioning the strength of the treatment control group comparison (Crawford, 1995). The study did not compare bilingual education with no bilingual education because two-thirds of the children in the control group had previously been in bilingual programs. In part because of the ambiguity of the conclusions from the AIR study, the other two major longitudinal studies discussed in this section were commissioned by the U.S. Department of Education in 1983 to look at program effectiveness.

[handwritten in left margin: Bad comparison gr.]

The Longitudinal Study

The Longitudinal Study had two distinct phases. The descriptive phase examined the variety of services provided to English-language learners in 86 schools. Some of its major findings were as follows:

• The vast majority of English-language learners came from economically disadvantaged families.
• English-language learners were at risk educationally, with most performing below grade level.
• Most instruction of the children was in English or in some combination of English and the native language.

The goal of the second phase of the study was a longitudinal follow-up to determine the relative effectiveness of programs. The focus was on 25 schools from the first phase, with both English-language learners and English-proficient students from kindergarten to fifth grade being followed over 3 years (Burkheimer et al., 1989). Because schools for the follow-up phase were initially selected on the basis of having representative populations of interest and not on the basis of program differences, there was not much variation in the programs represented in this phase. Moreover, some of the schools had no children in the control group. In an attempt to compensate for the weakness of the study design, elaborate statistical techniques were used. Given these limitations, one should be cautious about interpreting the study findings. The major findings can be summarized as follows (Burkheimer et al., 1989):

[handwritten marginalia: too short & of suf. lack of any projs.]

• Assignment of English-language learners to specific instructional services reflects principally local policy determinations. To a much more limited extent (mainly in the lower grades), assignment may be based on "deliberate" (and apparently criterion-driven) placement of students in the specific services for which they are ready.
• Too heavy a concentration in any one aspect of the English-language learner's education (e.g., reading) can detract from achievement in other areas (e.g., math or science).
• The yearly achievement of English-language learners in math and English-language arts is facilitated by different approaches, depending on student background factors. For example, students who are relatively English proficient are better able to benefit from English language arts instruction given in English, whereas students who are weak in English and/or strong in their native language eventually show better English language arts achievement when instructed in their native language.
• In the later grades, proficiency in mathematics when tested in English seems to require proficiency in English. This is not the case in the lower grades.

• As in the assignment of students to specific services for English-language learners, exit from those services reflects both local policy and specific criterion-driven exit rules related to reaching certain levels of proficiency/achievement in English.

• Children are more likely to be exited from English-language learner services if these services are similar to those for English-proficient students.

The Immersion Study (Ramírez)

The Immersion Study, conducted by Aguirre International, was a much more focused study of program alternatives than the Longitudinal Study. It attempted a quasi-experimental longitudinal comparison of three types of programs: English-only immersion, early-exit bilingual (also known as transitional bilingual), and late-exit bilingual (also known as maintenance bilingual). The study took place at nine sites, but five of these had only one of the three types of programs (Ramirez et al., 1991). In fact, the late-exit bilingual program was completely confounded with site, being the only program implemented at three sites. Despite sophisticated statistical models of growth, the conclusions from the study are seriously compromised by the noncomparability of sites.

noncomparability of sites

too short

The major findings of the comparison of program types were summarized by the U.S. Department of Education (1991). After 4 years in their respective programs, English-language learners in immersion strategy and early-exit programs demonstrated comparable skills in mathematics, language, and reading when tested in English. There were differences among the three late-exit sites in achievement level in the three subjects: students at the sites with the most use of Spanish and the most use of English ended sixth grade with the same skills in English language and reading; students at the two late-exit sites that used the most Spanish showed higher growth in mathematics skills than those at the site that abruptly transitioned into almost all-English instruction. Students in all three programs realized a growth in English-language and reading skills that was as rapid or more so than the growth that would have been expected for these children had they not received any intervention.

National Research Council Report

Both the Longitudinal and Immersion studies were reviewed by a National Research Council panel of the Committee on National Statistics

(Meyer and Fienberg, 1992). The primary focus of the panel's report is on determining whether the statistical methods used in those studies were appropriate. The report identified important flaws in these major efforts, including the following:

• The formal designs of the Longitudinal and Immersion studies were ill suited to answering the important policy questions that appear to have motivated them.

• Execution and interpretation of these studies, especially the Longitudinal Study, were hampered by a lack of documentation of the study objectives, the operationalizing of conceptual details, actual procedures followed, and changes in all of the above.

• Because of the poor articulation of study goals and the lack of fit between discernible goals and research design, it is unlikely that additional statistical analyses of the data would yield results central to the policy questions these studies were originally intended to address.

• Both the Longitudinal and Immersion studies suffered from excessive attention to the use of elaborate statistical methods intended to overcome the shortcomings in the research designs.

• Although the samples in the Immersion study were followed longitudinally, later comparisons are not considered valid because of sample attrition.

Quite clearly the Longitudinal and Immersion studies did not provide decisive evidence about the effectiveness of bilingual education programs. However, according to the National Research Council report, findings from the comparisons that were most sound with respect to study design and sample characteristics indicate that kindergarten and first grade students who received academic instruction in Spanish had higher achievement in reading in English (at kindergarten and grade 1) than comparable students who received academic instruction in English.

Reviews of Smaller-Scale Evaluations

Five key reviews of smaller-scale program evaluations were examined:

• Baker and de Kanter (1981) reviewed 28 studies of programs designed for English-language learners that reported evaluations considered to be methodologically sound.[1] Based on their review, they concluded that "the case for the effectiveness of transitional bilingual education is so weak that exclusive reliance on this instruction method is clearly not justified" (p. 1).

• Rossell and Ross (1986) and Rossell and Baker (1996) considered studies that evaluated alternative second-language programs. Their review included only studies that had random assignment to programs or statistical control for pretreatment differences between groups when random assignment was not possible. They concluded that the evidence from these studies did not support the superiority of transitional bilingual education for English-language learners.

• Willig (1985) conducted a meta-analysis of studies reviewed by Baker and de Kanter. In contrast with previous reviews, her analysis quantitatively measured the program effect in each study, even if it was not statistically significant. Her overall conclusion is quite different from that of the previous reviews: "positive effects for bilingual programs . . . for all major academic areas" (p. 297). However, as she notes, she did not compare bilingual education programs with other programs, but only contrasted program versus no-program studies.

• The U.S. General Accounting Office (1987) surveyed 10 experts in the field to gauge the effectiveness of bilingual education programs. Most of the experts surveyed looked quite favorably upon educational policy that encourages the use of the native language and were critical of structured immersion. Moreover, most questioned the value of "aggregate program labels" (e.g., immersion or transitional bilingual education) because such labels fail to capture fully the instructional activities and context at each site.

In summary, the beneficial effects of native-language instruction are clearly evident in programs that have been labeled "bilingual education," but they also appear in some programs that are labeled "bilingual immersion" (Gersten and Woodward, 1995). There appear to be benefits of programs that are labeled "structured immersion" (Baker and de Kanter, 1981; Rossell and Ross, 1986); however, a quantitative analysis of such programs is not yet available. Based primarily on the Willig (1985) meta-analysis, this report supports the conclusion of the previous National Re-

---

[1]To be considered methodologically sound, studies had to employ random assignment of children to treatment conditions or take measures to ensure that children in the treatment groups were equivalent. Studies with no comparison group were rejected.

search Council panel discussed earlier: "The panel still sees the elements of positive relationships that are consistent with empirical results from other studies and that support the theory underlying native language instruction" (Meyer and Fienberg, 1992:105).

However, for numerous reasons, we see little value in continuing to focus evaluations on the question of which type of program is best. First, the key to program improvement is not in finding a program that works for all children and all localities, but rather finding a set of program components that works for the children in the community of interest, given the goals, demographics, and resources of that community. The focus needs to be on the proper contexts in which a program component is most effective and conversely, the contexts in which it may even be harmful. Second, many large-scale evaluations would likely suffer from the problem encountered in some previous national evaluations: the programs would be so loosely implemented that the evaluation would have no clear focus. Third, programs are not unitary, but a complex series of components. Thus we think it better to focus on components than programs and on the needs of the local setting. As we argue later, successful bilingual and immersion programs may contain many common elements.

Politicization of Program Evaluation

It is difficult to synthesize the program evaluations of bilingual education because of the extreme politicization of the process. Research always involves compromises, and because no study is perfect, every study has weaknesses. What has happened in this area of research is that most consumers of the research are not researchers who want to know the truth, but advocates who are convinced of the absolute correctness of their positions. Advocates care mainly about the results of a study. If its conclusions support their position, they note the study's strong points; if not, they note its weak points. Because there are studies that support a wide range of positions, advocates on both sides end up with plenty of "evidence" to support their position. Policymakers are justifiably troubled by the inability of the research evidence to resolve the debate.

A related issue is that very quickly a new study gets labeled as pro- or anti-bilingual education. What is emphasized in the debate is not the quality of the research or insights about school and classroom attributes that contribute to or hinder positive student outcomes, but whether the study is consistent with the advocate's position. Because advocacy is the goal, very poor studies that support an advocated position are touted as definitive.

Future Course of Program Evaluation

It is easy to criticize previous program evaluations, but we need to realize that program evaluation was in its infancy when many of these studies were initially undertaken. During the past 25 years, the model of program evaluation has evolved considerably. There are several key elements in the current model (see Fetterman et al. [1995] for one such formulation). First, the initial focus is not on comparing programs, but on determining whether a given program is properly implemented and fine tuning it so it becomes more responsive to the needs of children, the school, and the community. Once the program has been established, a summative evaluation with control groups is recommended. Second, instead of being a top-down process, the evaluation is more participatory, guided by students, staff, and the community (Cousins and Earl, 1992). Third, qualitative as well as quantitative methods are used (see Chapter 4).

Although program evaluation to date has yielded disappointing results, it would be a serious mistake to say we have learned nothing from the enterprise. Five general lessons learned from the past 25 years of program evaluation follow.

Lesson 1: Higher-Quality Program Evaluations

The following factors are critical to high-quality program evaluations: program design, program implementation, creation of a control group, group equivalence, measurement, unit of analysis, power, and missing data.

Program Design   A program should have clearly articulated goals. Although scientific research can play a role in determining intermediate goals, program goals are generally determined by the school community. For instance, some communities may place a premium on students maintaining a native language, whereas others may prefer to encourage only the speaking of English. Once the program goals have been set, curriculum must be found or created, staffing requirements determined, and staff development procedures implemented. The program should be designed using basic theory (see the discussion of lesson 3 below), but should also be practical enough to be implemented in the schools.

Program Implementation   Many programs created for English-language learners by government, schools, researchers, and courts have not been fully implemented. An evaluation without evidence of successful implementation is an evaluation of an unknown quantity.

Demonstration of program implementation requires more than examining the educational background of teachers and the completion of forms filled out by administrators. While interviews with teachers and students can provide an approximate fix on what is actually being delivered, the best approach is to observe what teachers and students do in the classroom (see Chapter 7). Examining program implementation offers several advantages. First, it encourages thinking of the program not as unitary (e.g., bilingual education), but as a series of components; one can then determine whether each of these components has been implemented (see the discussion of lesson 4 below). Second, it allows for the measurement of processes that would otherwise not be measured, such as opportunity to learn. Third, if the implementation data are measured for the same children for whom outcome data are measured, it is possible to analyze the process by which program features are translated into outcomes.

Creation of a Control Group   Even when a program has clearly articulated goals, is based on sound theory, and is adequately implemented, a program evaluation is of little value if one does not know what experiences the children in the control group have had. Identifying control groups may be difficult. Because of legislative, judicial, and educational constraints, an untreated group may be difficult to find. Moreover, the researcher should not assume that just because children are not currently receiving an intervention, they never have. The current and past experiences of children in the control group need to be carefully documented.

One might suppose that an emphasis on standards precludes the need for a control group. While it may be important to examine whether students meet performance standards, we still need to know whether a program improves performance over what was achieved under a previous program. Moreover, given the economic background of most English-language learners (see Chapter 1) and the likely heavy English load in most testing (see Chapter 5), the use of standards could create an unduly pessimistic appraisal of these children. While high standards are the ultimate goal, they will likely have to be reached gradually.

Group Equivalence   Program evaluation involves comparison of an experimental and a control group. These two groups should be demographically and educationally equivalent. Equivalent groups are guaranteed by random assignment. Because of legislative, judicial, and administrative constraints, random assignment of students to conditions may not generally be feasible; nonetheless, we urge vigilance in attempting to find opportunities for random assignment. When random assignment is not feasible, other ways must be found to ensure that the groups are similar. As recommended by Meyer and Fienberg (1992), there is a greater likelihood of equivalence if the control group students can be selected from the same school. If another classroom, school, or school district must be chosen, it should be as similar as possible to the treated units.

Researchers need to ascertain whether the groups are equivalent before the intervention begins. The best way to do this is to measure the children in both groups to obtain a baseline measure. Ideally, there should be little or no difference at baseline.[2] If there are differences, statistical analysis can be used to make the groups more similar,[3] but it cannot be expected to make them truly equivalent.

Measurement The difficult issues of student assessment have already been discussed in Chapter 5. However, we note that longitudinal assessment of English-language learners virtually guarantees that different tests will be taken by different groups of children, making it necessary to equate the tests. The timing of measurement is important. The baseline or pretest measure should occur before the program begins, and the post-test should occur after the program has been completed and its potential effects are evident. A long interval from pretest to post-test will increase the amount of missing data in the sample (see below).

Unit of Analysis Even when there is random assignment, the child is generally not the unit assigned to the intervention, but rather the classroom, the school, or sometimes the district. A related issue is that children affect each other's learning in the classroom, and indeed, several recent educational innovations (e.g., cooperative learning) attempt to capitalize on this fact. Consideration then needs to be given to whether the child or some other entity is the proper unit of analysis.

Power This factor concerns the probability of detecting a difference between treatment and control groups if there actually is one. Program

---

[2]Ensuring equivalence by matching individual scores at the pretest only appears to create equivalence (Campbell and Stanley, 1963).

[3]There is considerable controversy about how to adjust statistically for baseline differences (e.g., Lord, 1967). This controversy reinforces the point that the presence of baseline differences seriously compromises the persuasiveness of the evaluation.

evaluations must be designed so that there is sufficient power. In many instances, there may be insufficient resources to achieve an acceptable level of power. For instance, there may be only 50 children eligible for a study, but to have a reasonable chance of getting a statistically reliable result may require more children in the sample. Even if there are sufficient resources, the study may be too large to manage.

Missing Data   Typically, evaluations are longitudinal, and in longitudinal research, missing data are always a serious concern. Given the high mobility of English-language learners, attrition is an especially critical issue in these types of evaluations (Lam, 1992). A plan for minimizing and estimating the effect of missing data should be attempted. To some extent, the use of growth-curve modeling (Bryk and Raudenbush, 1992) or the computation of individual change trajectories can alleviate this problem.

Summary   Clearly, program evaluations are difficult. The above discussion indicates that there are often tradeoffs: to maximize one aspect of a study, another must be reduced. Although research always involves compromises and limitations, there must still be some minimum degree of quality for the research to be informative. Therefore, sometimes the most prudent choice is not to conduct a program evaluation, but to devote research efforts to determining whether a program is successfully implemented in the classroom and identifying the process by which the program leads to desirable outcomes (see the discussion of lesson 2). At the same time, researchers and policymakers still need to be creative in recognizing opportunities for evaluation.

Lesson 2: More Informative Local Evaluations

Evaluation needs to be viewed as a tool for program improvement, not as a bureaucratic obligation. Local evaluation efforts need to focus on methods for improving program design and implementation (Ginsburg, 1992; Meyer and Fienberg, 1992). Lam (1992:193) makes the following recommendation: "It seems reasonable to urge local educators and administrators to use the majority of the evaluation budgets for formative purposes—that is, to document and guide full implementation of the program design, including the analysis of problems arising when the school's capacity to actually implement the proposed program is being developed."

Title VII legislation explicitly encourages this type of evaluation (Section 7123b).

Federal and state governments might monitor local evaluations more closely. School districts that present evidence for successfully implemented models should receive grants for outcome evaluation. While we do not believe in enforcing standardization across sites in these evaluations, there should be attempts to encourage collaboration that would allow pooling of results. There are successful examples in other areas of human resource evaluation in which there is local control, but comparable measures and designs are used to allow for data aggregation.

It should also be noted that both large-scale and local evaluations have their limitations. With smaller-scale evaluations, it is easier to monitor the effort, keep track of implementation, and institute procedures to minimize missing data. However, small evaluations are plagued with insufficient sample sizes and sometimes insufficient program variation. Moreover, results in one community may not be generalizable to other communities. Just as national evaluations were oversold in the 1970s and 1980s, we do not wish now to oversell local evaluations.

We expect program effects to interact with site and community characteristics.[4] Although some site effects will be random and inexplicable, others will be systematic. If enough sites can be studied, an understanding of the necessary conditions for successful programs can be developed. One statistical technique that is ideally suited for the analysis of within-site effects is hierarchical linear modeling (Bryk and Raudenbush, 1992), which can be used to test whether there are site interactions and determine what factors can explain them.

Lesson 3: Creation and Evaluation of Theory-Based Interventions

Programs should be designed so they are consistent with what is known about basic learning processes. The studies and programs described in this section are based on a theory of second-language learning and its relationship to student achievement and successful educational practice. The theory is tested through implementation in a classroom

---

[4]A good example of effects varying by site is presented by Samaniego and Eubank (1991). They tested basic theory using the California Case Studies in four school districts, and results varied considerably across sites.

setting. While none of the examples described here is perfect, each has aspects that are exemplary.

California Case Studies   In 1980, the California State Department of Education, in a collaboration with researchers and local educators, applied a theory-based model for bilingual education (Gold and Tempes, 1987). The program, which came to be known as the California Case Studies, began with a declaration of principles (see Chapter 7), many of which were based on research results reviewed in Chapters 2 through 4. Five elementary schools serving large numbers of Spanish-speaking students were selected for participation in the program. Students were provided substantial amounts of instruction in and through the native language; comprehensible second-language input was provided through both ESL classes and sheltered classes in academic content areas; and teachers attempted to equalize the status of second-language learners by treating English-language learners equitably, using cooperative learning strategies, providing second-language classes, and using minority languages for noninstructional purposes.

While the California Case Studies is exemplary in its application of principles based on well-established basic research and collaboration between educators and researchers, very few of its results have been published in peer-reviewed journals.[5]

Gersten's Bilingual Immersion Programs   In a series of studies published in peer-reviewed journals, Gersten and colleagues (Gersten, 1985; Gersten et al., 1984; Gersten and Woodward, 1995) tested the effectiveness of "bilingual immersion programs" for English-language learners. Gersten and Woodward (1995:226) define such a program as follows: "This approach retains the predominant focus on English-language instruction from the immersion model but tempers it with a substantive 4-year Spanish language program so that students maintain their facility with their native language." The program they developed is a blend of ideas from bilingual and immersion programs, hence their use of the term "bilingual immersion."[6]

---

[5]The program was never intended as an evaluation, and funding was cut at the end of the project, which made evaluation more difficult.

[6]Although Gersten and Woodward label this program "bilingual immersion," it should not be confused with two-way bilingual programs (also called "bilingual immersion programs"), in which native speakers of English and English-language learners are provided with subject matter instruction in their respective native language(s).

In a major 4-year study (Gersten and Woodward, 1995), 228 children in El Paso, Texas, were placed in either bilingual immersion (as defined above) or transitional bilingual programs. Children were followed from fourth through seventh grades. While differences found in language and reading ability in the early years favored the bilingual immersion approach, those differences seemed to vanish in the later years. However, almost all of the bilingual immersion children had been mainstreamed by the end of the program, while nearly one-third of the transitional bilingual children had not.[7]

Summary   Some of the examples in this section might be considered advocacy based. While there is very often a fine line between theory- and advocacy-based program evaluations, we see an important difference between the two. First, the former type of program is grounded in a theory about the learning of a second language and its relationship to student achievement, not solely in a social or political philosophy. Second, the educational curriculum is designed to implement the theory in a school setting. Third, the educational outcomes of children are used to test the theory; the program evaluation tests both the basic theory and the educational intervention.

Lesson 4: Thinking in Terms of Components, Not Political Labels

Historically, programs are described as unitary; a student is either in a program or not. The current debate on the relative efficacy of English immersion and bilingual education has been cast in this light. However, as noted above, we need to move away from thinking about programs in such broad terms and instead see them as containing multiple components—features that are available to meet the differing needs of particular students. Thus two students in the same program could receive different elements of the program. Moreover, programs that are nominally very different—especially the most successful ones—may have very similar characteristics (see Chapter 7). These common characteristics include the following:

---

[7]The statistical analysis of the data from this program by Gersten and Woodward (1995) has been less than optimal. Generally, analysis of variance is not appropriate for longitudinal studies. Moreover, growth curve analysis (Bryk and Raudenbush, 1992) can often provide a much more detailed picture of process. However, correcting these statistical problems would probably not result in major changes in the study's conclusions.

- Some native-language instruction, especially initially
- For most students, a relatively early phasing in of English instruction
- Teachers specially trained in instructing English-language learners

Lesson 5: Creation of a Developmental Model

A general formal model is needed to predict children's development of linguistic, social, and cognitive skills. The foundation of this model would be derived from basic research reviewed in Chapters 2 through 4, including theories of linguistic, cognitive, and social development. The model would predict nonlinear growth trajectories for the major abilities—not only the mean or typical trajectories, but also their variability. It would be flexible enough to allow for the introduction of a second language and would explicitly address possible transfer and interference for different first languages, as well as educational issues for new immigrants.

Learning takes place in specific environments, and these would be explicitly considered in the model as well. The environment would serve as a moderator that accelerates or decelerates the child's development. Among the school environment variables would be classroom composition, teachers, and school climate. Family and community variables would also serve as moderators. From a policy perspective, the most important moderators would be program inputs, for example, bilingual education and English immersion—not in an idealized sense, but in terms of instructional practices, such as percentage of first-language instruction. Moreover, the model would predict interactions between the effectiveness of program features and student and environmental characteristics.

The creation of such a model would require collaboration among researchers, statisticians, and educators. It would likely occur in stages. The model would be so complex that it would have to be computer simulated. It should be able not only to explain results that are currently well established, but also to make predictions about results that have not yet

---

[8]Findings from this study are not discussed in this report because the study had not been completed or published prior to the report's publication.

been obtained and those that are unexpected. The model would be much too large to be testable in its entirety, but should be specific enough to be testable in narrow contexts.

A research effort geared toward developing such a model is that of Thomas and Collier (1995).[8] Using data from the immersion studies discussed above and data collected since then from other school districts, Thomas and Collier sketch approximate growth curves for different programs. The model we envision would be much more extensive in that it would predict individual (as opposed to program) growth, as well as interactions between programs and child characteristics. Moreover, we would hope that programs in the model would be replaced by program features (see lesson 4).

IMPLICATIONS

The educational implications of the findings presented in this chapter correspond to the five lessons presented in the previous section.[9] First, higher-quality program evaluations are needed. Factors critical to high-quality program evaluations include sound program design, full program implementation, creation of a control group, group equivalence, adequate measurement, proper unit of analysis, enough power, and methods for dealing with missing data.

Second, local evaluations need to be made more informative. Further, they need to focus on methods for improving program design and implementation. Evaluation needs to be viewed as a tool for program improvement, not as a bureaucratic obligation.

Third, theory-based interventions need to be created and evaluated. Programs should be designed so they are consistent with what is known about basic learning processes. The studies and programs described in this chapter are based on a theory of second-language learning and its relationship to student achievement and successful educational practice. The theory is tested through implementation in a classroom setting.

Fourth, we need to move away from thinking about programs in broad terms and instead see them as containing multiple components—features that are available to meet the differing needs of particular students.

---

[9]This section does not present research implications because research is not needed on evaluation per se; rather, program evaluations need to be conducted differently if we are to learn from the programs and practices we implement.

Finally, a developmental model needs to be created for use in predicting the effects of program components on children in different environments. The foundation of this model would be derived from basic research reviewed in Chapters 2 through 4, including theories of linguistic, cognitive, and social development.

STUDIES OF SCHOOL AND CLASSROOM EFFECTIVENESS: KEY FINDINGS

The literature on school and classroom effectiveness provides the following key findings:

- The studies reviewed here provide some evidence to support the "effective schools" attributes identified nearly 20 years ago (strong leadership, high expectations for students, clear school-wide focus on basic skills, safe and orderly environment, and frequent assessment of student progress), with at least two important qualifications:
— The studies challenge the conceptualization of some of those attributes, for example, the idea that implementing characteristics of effective schools and classrooms makes schools and classrooms more effective.
— The studies suggest that factors not identified in the effective schools literature may be important as well if we are to create schools where English-language learners, indeed all students, will be successful and productive. Examples of such factors are a focus on more than just basics, ongoing staff development, and home-school connections.
- The following attributes are identified as being associated with effective schools and classrooms: a supportive school-wide climate, school leadership, a learning environment tailored to local goals and resources, articulation and coordination within and between schools, some use of native language and culture in the instruction of English-language learners, a balanced curriculum that incorporates both basic and higher-order skills, explicit skills instruction, opportunities for student-directed activities, use of instructional strategies that enhance understanding, opportunities for practice, systematic student assessment, staff development, and home and parent involvement.
- Although suggestive of key attributes that are important for creating effective schools and classrooms, most studies reviewed here cannot give firm answers about any particular attribute and its relationship to student outcomes. For example, the nominated schools designs do not report data on student outcomes and are thus inconclusive. Prospective case studies lack comparison groups, so that changes in student outcomes may be due to extraneous factors. And while quasi-experimental studies that focus on an entire program provide the strongest basis for claims about program or school effects, they make direct claims only about the program or school effect overall. Claims about the effects of specific components must, in general, rest on other studies that examine those components explicitly.

7

Studies of School and Classroom Effectiveness

Whereas Chapter 6 focuses on program evaluations, in which the issue of instructional language is paramount, this chapter focuses on empirical studies that attempt to identify school- and classroom-level factors related to effective schooling for English-language learners from early education programs through high school. Although the issue of language of instruction is an important feature of the research described in this chapter, it does not dominate the work as much as it has the evaluation research discussed in Chapter 6.

FINDINGS

Observations on Studies of Effective Schools and Classrooms

Based on a systematic literature search, we identified reports of 33 studies for inclusion in this review (see the appendix). Several general observations can be made about this collection. First, this is a heterogeneous group of studies, employing at least four different types of designs. In the effective schools design, schools are designated as effective based on measures of student learning or achievement. In the nominated schools design, schools are identified in accordance with the professional judgments of knowledgeable educators, rather than being identified on the basis of outcome measures. Prospective case studies and quasi-experiments represent a different approach to studying effective schooling. Instead of finding schools that are already "effective" or have been nominated as such, prospective studies attempt to document changes in school-wide programs or classrooms and the effects of these changes on student achievement. Quasi-experimental designs employ comparison schools or classrooms. In addition, the studies range from single-classroom and -school studies to a study of nine different "exemplary programs" in a total of 39 schools. Furthermore, they represent levels of schooling from kindergarten to preschool.

A second general observation is that school- and classroom-level factors associated with varying outcomes for English-language learners have received less attention than have other areas of research on these students. Clearly, the issue of language of instruction (whether English-language learners should be taught in their native language, and if so, to what extent) has dominated the research agenda (see Chapter 6). There have also been qualitative and ethnographic studies that have examined social context, language distribution, classroom interaction, and sociocultural enactments of classroom pedagogy (see Chapters 2-4). Although these studies provide rich descriptions of educational environments, many do not relate practice to learning outcomes.

Third, although many non-English languages found in U.S. schools appear to be represented in these studies, by far the most commonly found is Spanish. This of course reflects the reality that approximately three-fourths of English-language learners are Spanish speaking. Most of the studies were conducted in schools that were predominately Latino. However, some sites within larger studies had substantial numbers of non-Spanish-speaking English-language learners. Only a few studies—Slavin and Yampolsky (1992) (Asian), Wong Fillmore et al. (1985) (Chinese), Rosebery et al. (1992) (Haitian-Creole), and Tharp (1982) (Hawaiian)—targeted non-Spanish-speaking English-language learners.

Fourth, as previously mentioned, by far the greatest number of schools and classrooms studied have been within the nominated schools design. These studies, as well as a few in the other categories, do not report student achievement data.[1] The absence of outcome data does not mean

---

[1] In their report on the California Case Studies, Gold and Tempes (1987:7) explicitly state that their project "was not designed as an experiment" and that they "carefully avoided efforts to set up premature or unreasonable comparisons." However, achievement data on the California Case Studies have been reported in various papers and publications (e.g., Krashen and Biber, 1988). Samaniego and Eubank (1991) conducted a more objective and rigorous secondary analysis of achievement data at four of the five sites. Three other studies included in this review (Lucas et al., 1990; Tikunoff, 1983; Tikunoff et al., 1991) report that some indicators of student outcomes informed the selec-

that a study is uninformative. Indeed, these studies are filled with interesting and useful data about programs, staff, students, community, and, more generally, the very complex and challenging circumstances in which students and teachers must function. They also provide what in many cases are highly compelling accounts of dedicated educators working to create engaging, meaningful, and responsive settings for student learning. However, they do not link these settings to indicators of student outcomes, at least not in any explicit way.

Finally, as noted above, these studies report a wide range of school- and classroom-level attributes related to effectiveness. These attributes, summarized in the following section, can be conceptualized and categorized in many different ways. It is important to keep in mind, however, that the attributes discussed here represent concepts refracted through at least two sets of lenses (the original investigators' and this committee's), that the empirical bases for making strong causal claims vary considerably and are sometimes unknown, and that there are caveats associated with some of the attributes. For example, different attributes may be more or less important for different age groups or different ethnic groups. Therefore, none of these individual attributes should be considered necessary or sufficient conditions for the schooling of English-language learners.

Attributes of Effective Schools and Classrooms

Based on the findings of the 33 studies reviewed, effective schools and classrooms can be said to have the following attributes.[2]

Supportive School-Wide Climate

Carter and Chatfield (1986), Moll (1988), Lucas et al. (1990), Tikunoff (1983), Tikunoff et al. (1991), Berman et al. (1992, 1995), and Minicucci

---

tion of the "effective" or "exemplary" sites, but neither these data nor the criteria used by investigators are reported. Of the remaining studies, one was exclusively exploratory (Minicucci and Olsen, 1992) and makes no claim of trying to explain how effective programs came to be; the studies by Berman et al. (1992, 1995), Pease-Alvarez et al. (1991), and Gersten (1996) neither report outcome data nor apparently used student outcomes to inform the selection of nominated sites. With the exception of Short (1994), which is more of an exploratory study, the prospective and quasi-experimental studies report student outcome data.

[2]Note that not all studies include all attributes, but the general attributes appear in many of the studies.

and Olsen (1992) report that a positive school-wide climate was a feature of the effective or exemplary schools they studied. The schools varied in their particular manifestations of such a climate, but overall emphasized three things—value placed on the linguistic and cultural background of English-language learners, high expectations for their academic achievement, and their integral involvement in the overall school operation.

How does a school climate, or ethos, change from being "not conducive" to being "conducive" to high levels of achievement for English-language learners? Unfortunately, the studies do not offer much guidance here. Only Goldenberg and Sullivan (1994) address this question directly and prospectively. They claim that changes in school climate were the result of a complex process, aimed at improving student achievement, that began with identification of school-wide goals and expectations for students, followed by consistent, visible, multiple, and long-term efforts to work toward those goals. Teachers responded positively to the more meaningful and substantive focus at the school.

Although the logic of attempting to change school climate through staff development and training to improve student achievement is supported by research on teacher expectations, an alternative hypothesis may merit attention: that school climate is at least as much a reflection of student achievement as an influence on it (Jussim, 1986). In other words, it may be that teachers hold high expectations when they have students who achieve, and conversely that they hold low expectations when their students do not achieve. If this formulation is valid, it suggests that one important way to raise teacher expectations is to increase student achievement by creating structures at a school and helping teachers acquire the skills and knowledge needed to be more successful with students, rather than by exhorting teachers to raise their expectations.

School Leadership

Consistent with findings of the effective schools research that began two decades ago, school-level leadership appears to be a critical dimension of effective schooling for English-language learners (Tikunoff et al., 1991; Carter and Chatfield, 1986; Lucas et al., 1990; Goldenberg and Sullivan, 1994). At least half of the studies reviewed name leadership, often the principal's, as an important factor; the role of leadership can also be inferred from several of the other studies that do not explicitly cite it.

An important exception can be found in the Success for All studies, which do not name leadership as an important attribute. This stance is atypical of the school change literature as a whole, and some suggest that the Success for All program does not require a strong principal because leadership comes from a Success for All site facilitator, teachers provide this leadership, and the program is highly structured and limited to language arts and reading instruction.

Customized Learning Environment

Staff in effective schools and classrooms design the learning environment to reflect school and community contextual factors and goals while meeting the diverse needs of their students (Berman et al., 1992, 1995; Tikunoff et al., 1991; Moll, 1988; Samaniego and Eubank, 1991; Lucas et al., 1990). Many researchers have noted that there is no one right way to educate English-language learners; different approaches are necessary because of the great diversity of conditions faced by schools and students. These researchers recommend that local staff and community members identify the conditions under which one or some combination of approaches is best suited and then adapt models to match their particular circumstances. For example, Lucas et al. (1990) found that English-language learners are more likely to achieve when a school's curriculum responds to their individual and differing needs by offering variety in three areas: the skills, abilities, and knowledge classes are designed to develop (i.e., native-language development, ESL, subject matter knowledge); the degrees of difficulty and sophistication among available classes (i.e., advanced as well as low-level classes); and the approaches to teaching content (i.e., native-language instruction, content ESL, and specially designed instruction in English).

Articulation and Coordination Within and Between Schools

Effective schools are characterized by a smooth transition between levels of language development classes (e.g., between content-based ESL and sheltered instruction) and coordination and articulation between special second-language programs and other school programs, as well as between levels of schooling (Short, 1994; Slavin and Yampolsky, 1992; Minicucci and Olsen, 1992; Berman et al., 1995; Saunders et al., 1996; Calderon et al., 1996). In many of the schools studied, there was collaboration between special language teachers and mainstream classroom or content teachers to articulate students' instructional programs. Moreover, in these schools the transition from special language instruction to mainstream classes was gradual, carefully planned, and supported with activities (prior to reclassification and after mainstreaming) designed to ensure students' success.

Use of Native Language and Culture

The advantages of native-language use are a prominent theme among these studies, either explicitly (e.g., Henderson and Landesman, 1992; Hernandez, 1991; Muniz-Swicegood, 1994; Lucas et al., 1990; Berman et al., 1995; Rosebery et al., 1992, Tikunoff, 1983; Pease-Alvarez et al., 1991; Calderon et al., 1996) or implicitly (Carter and Chatfield, 1986, and Goldenberg and Sullivan, 1994, both of which took place in school settings where there was a firm commitment to bilingual education). Even those studies that report on Special Alternative Instructional Programs, where most instruction takes place in English, cite teachers' use of students' native languages to clarify and elaborate on points made in English (Tikunoff et al., 1991). Moreover, findings from a study of nine Special Alternative Instructional Programs (Lucas and Katz, 1994:545) indicate that even in exemplary programs designed to provide instruction primarily in English, the classrooms were "multilingual environments in which students' native languages served a multitude of purposes and functions. Across sites, native language use emerged as a persistent and key instructional strategy realized in very site-specific ways."

Nevertheless, several sites examined in these studies do not feature native-language programs. One of the Success for All sites, for example, has a largely Asian population, and all instruction is in English. In addition, while some of the Spanish-speaking students in the Success for All studies are in primary-language programs, some are in sheltered English programs.

Similarly, most of the studies cited in this review can contribute little direct knowledge to important questions about adapting instructional programs to students' home culture (e.g., sociolinguistic patterns, cognitive styles). These studies take place in contexts where the students' home culture is valued and seen as a resource to build upon, rather than a liability to remediate. Most of the studies report some aspect of home culture validation, accommodation, or inclusion in their effective sites.

Again, Success for All presents a challenging counterpoint. There is nothing in the Success for All literature indicating that cultural validation or cultural accommodation per se is an important element of the program or, indeed, that culture plays any direct role at all (aside from language). Of course, it is possible that cultural adaptations were taking place in the

Success for All schools studied (as a result of the programs or not), but this factor was not examined.

Thus the studies reviewed can, at best, make an oblique contribution to the debate on the role of home language and culture in the education of these students. In part, this is because there are no rigorous studies that have controlled for interactions among student background (e.g., prior schooling in the native language, age), ways in which the first and second languages are used, and other instructional variables (e.g., overall quality of schooling).

Balanced Curriculum

In much of the quasi-experimental research, classroom teachers combine basic and higher-order skills. In the Success for All schools, there is a balance between instruction in basic and higher-order skills at all grade levels. Success for All's strong outcomes make the balance of these two levels of instruction very compelling. Both Goldenberg and Gallimore (1991) and Goldenberg and Sullivan (1994) report that the schools they worked with and studied included a "balanced" literacy program in which key skills and subjects such as phonics, word recognition, specific comprehension skills, and writing conventions were taught. However, they argue that early reading achievement improved at those schools partly because teachers incorporated language and meaning-based approaches into a system that had previously relied on basic decoding skills as the only avenue for learning to read.

Explicit Skills Instruction

The studies reviewed indicate that effective teachers for English-language learners use explicit skills instruction for certain tasks, mostly (though not always) to help students acquire basic skills (Wong Fillmore et al., 1985; Tikunoff, 1983; Carter and Chatfield, 1986; Goldenberg and Sullivan, 1994; Slavin and Yampolosky, 1992). The value of explicit skills instruction is corroborated by other researchers. According to Sternberg (1986), explicit skills instruction is highly effective for some tasks (e.g., teaching subject matter knowledge, knowledge of hierarchical relationships among bits of information, and knowledge of valid strategies in science, and enhancing beginning readers' ability to decode and use process strategies such as summarization, clarification, questioning, and prediction to enhance comprehension). Executive processes such as comprehension monitoring can also be taught through explicit skills instruction if developmentally appropriate for the student. Rosenshine and Stevens (1986) argue that explicit teaching is highly effective for well-structured skill and knowledge domains such as math computation, explicit reading comprehension strategies, map reading, and decoding.

Opportunities for Student-Directed Activities

The studies reviewed indicate that teachers supplement explicit skills instruction, characteristic of the initial effective schools research, with student-directed activities such as cooperative learning, partner reading, and collaborative inquiry (Berman et al., 1995; Moll, 1988; Pease-Alvarez et al., 1991; Rosebery et al., 1992; Henderson and Landesman, 1992; Cohen, 1984; Muniz-Swicegood, 1994; Hernandez, 1991; Calderon et al., 1996; Saunders et al., 1996; Gersten, 1996).

Instructional Strategies That Enhance Understanding

Effective teachers of English-language learners use specially tailored strategies to enhance understanding. Examples include teaching metacognitive strategies (Dianda and Flaherty, 1995; Muniz-Swicegood, 1994; Hernandez, 1991; Chamot et al., 1992) and using routines (Edelsky et al., 1983; Calderon et al., 1996). Making instruction comprehensible to English-language learners by adjusting the level of English vocabulary and structure so it is appropriate for the students given their current level of proficiency in English is another important strategy and entails the following: using explicit discourse markers such as "first" and "next"; calling attention to the language in the course of using it; using the language in ways that reveal its structure; providing explicit discussion of vocabulary and structure; explaining and in some cases demonstrating what students will be doing or experiencing; providing students with appropriate background knowledge; building on students' previous knowledge and understanding to establish a connection between personal experience and the subject matter they are learning; and using manipulatives, pictures, objects, and film related to the subject matter (Wong Fillmore et al., 1985; Gersten 1996; Mace-Matluck et al., 1989; Saunders et al., 1996; Short, 1994).

Opportunities for Practice

This attribute entails building redundancy into activities, giving English-language learners opportunities to interact with fluent English-speaking peers, and providing opportunities for extended dialogue (Saunders et al., 1996; Calderon et al., 1996; Berman et al., 1995; Wong Fillmore et al., 1985; Tikunoff et al., 1991; Garcia, 1990a; Gersten, 1996). One method of providing opportunity for extended dialogue is the "instructional conversation"—discussion-based lessons focused on an idea or concept that has both educational value and meaning and relevance for students. The teacher encourages students to express their ideas either orally or in writing not just to the teacher, but also to classmates, and guides them to increasingly sophisticated levels of understanding (Saunders et al., 1996; Saunders and Goldenberg, in press).

Systematic Student Assessment

Many studies have found that effective schools use systematic student assessment—a feature identified in the effective and nominated schools research—to inform ongoing efforts to improve achievement (Carter and Chatfield, 1986; Goldenberg and Gallimore, 1991; Goldenberg and Sullivan, 1994; Slavin and Yampolsky, 1992; Slavin and Madden, 1994). In these schools, students are assessed on a regular basis to determine whether they need additional or different assistance; programmatic changes are made on this basis. (See also Chapter 5.)

Staff Development

Staff training and development are important components of effective schools for English-language learners not identified in the original effective schools research. As previously mentioned, one important way to raise teacher expectations is to increase student achievement by helping teachers acquire the skills and knowledge needed to be more successful with students, rather than exhorting teachers to raise their expectations. Often the training identified in the studies reviewed here is specific to teachers of these students, such as English-language development and use of sheltered instruction (Lucas et al., 1990). In other instances (e.g., Slavin and Yampolsky, 1992; Slavin and Madden, 1994), the training is in instructional strategies that are specific to the implemented program, such as use of thematic units, vocabulary development, classroom management, instructional pace, and cooperative learning, but not targeted at English-language learners per se.

Staff development for all teachers in the school, not just language specialists, was an important component of many of these programs (Carter and Chatfield, 1986; Lucas et al., 1990; Minicucci and Olsen, 1992; Berman et al., 1995). Although the programs provided ongoing staff development directly related to resolving new instructional issues for ESL and bilingual education teachers, they also recruited excellent content area teachers and trained them in English-language development strategies.

In preparing teachers, Moll and his colleagues (Moll et al., 1992) have avoided one pitfall often associated with culturally responsive pedagogy (defined as teaching practices attuned to the cultural background of students)—the tendency to base instructional practices on teachers' assumptions and stereotypical beliefs about groups of students. They base professional development on empirical findings about the community, rather than stereotypes.

A real question that remains is what sort of training is most relevant for improving school processes, as well as teacher knowledge and skills. It is also important to validate the effectiveness of this training through assessments of student outcomes.

Home and Parent Involvement

Home and parent involvement—an attribute that, like staff development, was not a part of the original effective schools conceptualization—plays an important role in enhancing outcomes for English-language learners. Moll (1988), Garcia (1990b), Carter and Chatfield (1986), and Lucas et al. (1990) all note that in the effective schools they document, an ongoing community/school process is an important contributor to the school's success.

Neither the studies reviewed here nor any other existing studies can answer the question of what type of home or parent involvement is most effective. Extrapolating from the observations in these studies, however, two hypotheses seem reasonable. First, cognitive or academic effects are most likely to be the result of home-school connections that focus specifically on cognitive or academic learning at home, that is, increasing and improving home learning opportunities through the use of homework or other organized activities designed to promote learning. Second, schools with comprehensive home involvement programs encompassing various types of home-school connections probably help families and children in a number of important ways. The more types of productive connections homes and schools can forge, the more positive and powerful the effects on children, families, and schools will be. At least in U.S. settings, these hypotheses are probably valid regardless of students' cultural or language background (Goldenberg, 1993). (See Chapter 4 for further elaboration on this theme.)

Methodological Strengths and Limitations of the Studies

Each of the major types of studies reviewed here has its methodological strengths and limitations. While the fact that a study has limitations does not invalidate its findings, those limitations should be considered in assessing the strength and generalizability of its conclusions. The nominated schools and classroom designs have introduced a valuable element to the literature—rich and highly detailed descriptions, some quantitative and some qualitative, of schools and classrooms. As exploratory strategies, both the effective and nominated schools designs make a great deal of intuitive and logical sense. But there are also limitations to what they can tell us. First, and most fundamental, neither design directly or empirically addresses the issue of how a school or classroom came to be effective, except for possible retrospective accounts and inferences. A second limitation of these designs, related to the first, is the difficulty of separating cause from effect: Do the characteristics of schools cause them to be effective, or does effectiveness lead to these characteristics? As previously mentioned, a third limitation is that the nominated schools design now in favor reports no data whatsoever on student outcomes, although some gauge of student outcomes may have been used in the selection process. Exemplary schools are selected because they satisfy criteria shared by nominators and investigators regarding what effective schooling for English-language learners should look like.

Prospective case studies have the advantage, in principle, of collecting data contemporaneously with change efforts, permitting observation and analysis of the actual change process, participants' views and perspectives, and the apparent ongoing results of the changes undertaken. Under ideal circumstances, they would be true cases of the implementation of theories regarding effective schooling. However, our systematic review uncovered very few such studies beyond those described in the previous section. An advantage of these studies, from a purely pragmatic standpoint, is that if the changes are effective and actually work, the students and teachers at the intervention site will have benefited. However, methodological problems, possibly related to the close collaboration of researchers and educators, can compromise study findings. For example, in one study, investigators who analyzed the interview protocols for changes in student knowledge knew which protocols were pretest and which were post-test.

Traditionally, threats to validity have been addressed within an experimental framework or, when dealing with social phenomena where random assignment is impossible, a quasi-experimental framework. From a design standpoint, the quasi-experimental design obviously offers a stronger basis for claiming that changes in student achievement resulted from something that happened at a target site. In the absence of a comparison site with students who are comparable in features such as demographics and transience, changes in student outcomes at a particular school can be due to any number of extraneous factors or artifacts. Quasi-experiments also permit stronger causal inferences about school processes, dynamics, and structures on the one hand and improvements in student outcomes on the other.

However, school changes are so complex and involve so many dimensions that it is usually very difficult to draw tight linkages between specific processes or program components and student outcomes. Quasi-experimental designs are really just parallel case studies and do not preclude in-depth study and subtle analysis of school and instructional organization features. On the contrary, richer descriptions of the processes and dynamics of school change would permit clearer interpretations or hypotheses about what explains changes in student outcomes—or the failure to effect such changes. Quasi-experimental designs do require that investigators either take an active hand in helping to bring about changes at a school or be present when a school, on its own, decides to try to instigate changes so that appropriate measures in the "before" state can be taken. In either case, investigators must then gauge the effects of those changes on student outcomes, using appropriate measures and comparable schools as controls.

Some of the studies reviewed here—particularly those that examine student outcomes and relate them to changes in school-wide and classroom functioning and organization—suggest processes by which schools and classrooms can reorganize themselves to promote higher levels of achievement for students. An important question is whether a school can become effective by successfully adopting an effective externally developed program, or a certain amount of "reinventing the wheel" is required, school by school. Although Slavin and Madden's (1995) results provide a strong basis for concluding that some well-defined effective programs can be exported successfully, their position (and, apparently, their data) runs counter not only to much of the accepted wisdom in the school reform literature, but also to previous efforts to disseminate and replicate effective programs (e.g., Anderson et al., 1978).

IMPLICATIONS

Educational

A number of attributes have been discussed in this chapter that are identified as being associated with effective schools and classrooms. Although these attributes provide important guidance for developing effective programs and instructional strategies for English-language learners, they need to be assessed in the context of the schools and classrooms in which they are implemented. To determine their effectiveness, it is critical to know the extent to which they have been implemented and to measure associated student outcomes.

Research

Researchers should make explicit their principles for selecting effective schools and classrooms. These principles should be based on some combination of indicators of process (e.g., curriculum, leadership, school climate, instructional strategies) and outcomes (e.g., standardized and performance-based achievement measures). The definition should be influenced by local priorities and contexts. In addition, research should investigate the extent of variability in the definition of effective schools and classrooms for English-language learners, for example, how definitions of effectiveness interact with local site characteristics and student characteristics.

Once learning goals have been set by the community, research is needed to determine the linguistic and cultural adaptations that will help English-language learners meet these goals. What methods work best to give English-language learners access to the academic and social opportunities of native English speakers? Such methods include both school-wide adaptations, such as the way sequences of classes are organized to give English-language learners optimal access to subject matter knowledge and English proficiency, and classroom adaptations, such the use of particular teaching strategies and classroom composition. Moreover, research is needed to determine the resources required for effective instruction of English-language learners in different contexts.

Research is needed as well to examine effective educational practice for special populations: (1) the effects of instructional interventions and social environments on the linguistic, social, and cognitive development of young children; (2) the attributes of effective middle and secondary schools and classrooms serving English-language learners; and (3) the effectiveness of newcomer programs, either in relationship to each other or compared with doing nothing at all.

Involving families of English-language learners and engaging community resources on their behalf pose special challenges for schools. More focused research is needed to provide information about the challenges to such involvement and engagement, the potential benefits, and successful approaches.

Prospective research that examines the school change process is also needed, beginning from the point before a school undertakes change, to document the processes and outcomes on a sound theoretical and programmatic basis. Prospective studies should document the problems, possibilities, dynamics, difficulties, successes, and outcomes of school and program change. An important focus should be on how schools and teachers maintain effective components once in place. Research should also determine which kinds of improvement strategies are exportable and which aspects may be influenced by local context.

In addition, future research should examine the benefits and shortcomings of different improvement strategies, again using models and programs already in existence. A component of this research should be to examine whether educators and policymakers find empirical research or rich cases more compelling in prompting them to change their current practices. Some prospective case studies of sites on the verge of reform could help answer these important policy implementation questions.

Finally, research should examine the extent to which generic reform efforts incorporate English-language learners. Moreover, this research should explore whether these reform efforts are beneficial to English-language learners, and if not how they can be adapted to benefit this group of students.

APPENDIX
STUDIES OF SCHOOL AND CLASSROOM EFFECTIVENESS

Effective Schools

Carter and Chatfield (1986)

Effective Classrooms

Edelsky et al. (1983)
Mace-Matluck et al. (1989)
Wong Fillmore et al. (1985)

Effective and Nominated Classrooms

Garcia (1990a)
Moll (1988)

Nominated Schools

Berman et al. (1995)
Berman et al. (1992)
Gersten (1966)
Lucas et al. (1990)
Pease-Alvarez et al. (1991)
Tikunoff et al. (1991)
Tikunoff (1983)

Prospective Case Studies

Cohen (1984)
Gold and Tempes (1987)
Hernandez (1991)
Rosebery et al. (1992)
Short (1994)

Quasi-Experimental Studies

Calderon et al. (1996)
Chamot et al. (1992)
Dianda and Flaherty (1994)
Goldenberg and Sullivan (1994)
Goldenberg and Gallimore (1991)
Henderson and Landesman (1992)
Muniz-Swicegood (1994)
Saunders et al. (1996)
Slavin and Madden (1994)
Slavin and Yampolsky (1992)

Experimental

Tharp (1982)

Other

Minicucci and Olsen (1992)

Concluding Remarks

This report has reviewed research in a broad range of substantive areas, with a focus on how best to meet the academic and social needs of English-language learners: how students learn a second language; how multiple languages are used and organized by bilingual children; how reading and writing skills develop in the first and second language; how information in specific content areas, such as mathematics and history, is learned and stored; how social and motivational factors affect learning among language-minority groups; how relations between different racial or ethnic groups are structured and moderated in school settings; how parents and communities influence and support learning; how student English proficiency and knowledge of content areas can be appropriately assessed; how programs can be evaluated with regard to achieving their goals; and how school and classroom characteristics influence learning.

Knowledge useful to the successful education of English-language learners has accumulated differentially across these areas. Some topics, such as second-language acquisition and conversational patterns in bilingual settings, have been characterized by a cumulative progression of theories and data. The challenge in these areas, then, is to extend the research to new languages, to new aspects of language, and to new subpopulations of research subjects. Other topics, such as the learning of academic content areas, have seen important developments in the mainstream research literature, but these insights have not been extended to language-minority populations. Others, such as program evaluation and effective schools, have seen significant activity, but a serious redirection of current efforts is warranted. Still others are plainly important, yet a major effort to address the fundamental issues for English-language learners has yet to be mounted; these topics include second-language literacy, intergroup relations, and the social context of learning.

We envision a model of instruction that is grounded in basic knowledge about the linguistic, cognitive, and social development of language-minority children. This model would be rich enough to suggest different programs for different types of students. The formulation of such a model would take time, and the participation of researchers from very different backgrounds, working collaboratively with practicing educators, would be required. Yet this model could serve as the basis for designing programs that would result in better outcomes for students.

As this summary report has shown, considerable knowledge has already accrued, and as the full report indicates, there are many ways of strengthening and building on this knowledge. Our vision can be realized only through a strategic combination of theory, research, program development, evaluation, and monitoring. We hope that the review presented here will be useful to all those interested in improving the education of language-minority children.

References

CHAPTER 1
OVERVIEW

Christian, D., and A. Whitcher
    1995   *Directory of Two-Way Bilingual Programs in the United States.* Revised. Santa Cruz, CA, and Washington, DC: National Center for Research on Cultural Diversity and Second Language Learning.

Education Week
    1996   Enrollment crunch stretches the bounds of the possible. *Education Week* (September 11):1.

Fleischman, H.L., and P.J. Hopstock
    1993   *Descriptive Study of Services to Limited English Proficient Students, Volume 1. Summary of Findings and Conclusions.* Arlington, VA: Development Associates.

Hopstock, P.J., and B.J. Bucaro
    1993   *A Review and Analysis of Estimates of the LEP Student Population.* Arlington, VA: Development Associates, Special Issues Analysis Center.

McArthur, E.K.
    1993   *Language Characteristics and Schooling in the United States, A Changing Picture: 1979 and 1989.* National Center for Education Statistics, Office of Educational Research and Improvement. Document number NCES 93-699. Washington, DC: U.S. Government Printing Office.

Moss, M., and M. Puma
    1995   *Prospects: The Congressionally Mandated Study of Educational Growth and Opportunity.* Cambridge, MA: Abt.

Ramirez, D.J., S.D. Yuen, D.R. Ramey, and D.J. Pasta
   1991   *Final Report: National Longitudinal Study of Structured-English Immersion Strategy, Early-Exit and Late-Exit Transitional Bilingual Education Programs for Language-Minority Children. Volumes I and II.* San Mateo, CA: Aguirre International.
Rivera, C.
   1994   Is it real for all kids? *Harvard Educational Review* 64(1):55-75.
Sheppard, K.
   1995   *Content-ESL Across the USA: A Technical Report.* Final report submitted to the Office of Bilingual Education and Minority Languages Affairs, U.S. Department of Education. Washington, DC: Center for Applied Linguistics.

CHAPTER 2
BILINGUALISM AND SECOND-LANGUAGE LEARNING

Baetens-Beardsmore, H.
   1986   *Bilingualism: Basic Principles.* 2nd ed. Clevedon, England: Tieto.
Bialystok, E., and K. Hakuta
   1994   *In Other Words.* New York: Basic Books.
Bruck, M.
   1982   Language-disabled children performance in additive bilingual education programs. *Applied Psycholinguistics* 3:45-60.
   1984   Feasibility of an additive bilingual program for the language impaired child. In Y. LeBrun and M. Paradis, eds., *Early Bilingualism and Child Development.* Amsterdam: Swets and Zeitlinger.
Campos, S.J.
   1995   The Carpinteria Preschool Program: A long-term effects study. In E. Garcia and B. McLaughlin, eds., *Meeting the Challenge of Linguistic and Cultural Diversity in Early Childhood Education.* New York: Teacher's College.
Carnegie Corporation
   1996   *Years of Promise. A Comprehensive Learning Strategy for America's Children.* New York: Carnegie Corporation.
Carroll, J.B.
   1986   Second language. Pp. 83-125 in R.F. Dillon and R.J. Sternbery, eds., *Cognition and Instruction.* Orlando, FL: Academic Press.
Collier, V.P.
   1987   Age and rate acquisition of second language for academic purposes. *TESOL Quarterly* 21(4):617-641.
Cummins, J.
   1984   *Bilingualism and Special Education.* San Diego, CA: College Hill Press.
Duncan, S., and E. DeAvila
   1979   Bilingualism and cognition: Some recent findings. *NABE Journal* 4:15-50.
Ellis, R.
   1984   Communication strategies and the evaluation of communicative performance. *ELT Journal* 38(1):39-44.

Enright, B.E.
1982   Criterion-referenced Tests: A Guide to Separate Useful from Useless. Paper presented at the Annual International Convention of the Council for Exceptional Children, Houston, TX, April 11-16; Session T-27. University of North Carolina at Charlotte.

Epstein, S.D., D. Flynn, and G. Martohardjono
1996   Second language acquisition: Theoretical and experimental issues in contemporary research. *The Behavioral and Brain Sciences* 19(4):677-758.

Fishman, J.A.
1978   *Advances in the Study of Societal Multilingualism.* The Hague, The Netherlands, and New York: Mouton.

Fishman, J.A., V. Nahirny, J. Hofman, and R. Hayden
1966   *Language Loyalty in the United States: The Maintenance and Perpetuation of Non-English Mother Tongues by American Ethnic and Religious Groups.* The Hague: Mouton.

Galambos, S.J., and K. Hakuta
1988   Subject-specific and task-specific characteristics of metalinguistic awareness in bilingual children. *Applied Psycholinguistics* 9(2):141-162.

Gardner, R.C.
1983   Learning another language: A true social psychological experiment. *Journal of Language and Social Psychology* 2:219-239.

Genesee, F., J. Hamers, W. Lambert, L. Mononen, M. Seitz, and R. Starck
1978   Language processing in bilinguals. *Brain and Language* 5:1-12.

Genesse, F.
1992   Second/foreign language immersion and at-risk English-speaking children. *Foreign Language Annals* 25:199-213.

Grosjean, F.
1982   *Life with Two Languages.* Cambridge, MA: Harvard University Press.

Hakuta, K.
1986   *Mirror of Language: The Debate on Bilingualism.* New York: Basic Books.
1987   Degree of bilingualism and cognitive ability in mainland Puerto Rican children. *Child Development* 58(5):1372-1388.

Hakuta, K., and D. D'Andrea
1992   Some properties of bilingual maintenance and loss in Mexican background high-school students. *Applied Linguistics* 13(1):72-99.

Hamers, J., and M. Blanc
1989   *Bilingualism and Bilinguality.* Cambridge, England, and New York: Cambridge University Press.

Harley, B., and W. Wang
1997   The critical period hypothesis: Where are we now? In A.M.B. de Groot and J.F. Kroll, eds., *Tutorials in Bilingualism: Psycholinguistic Perspectives.* Hillsdale, NJ: Erlbaum.

Klein, W.
1986   *Second Language Acquisition.* Cambridge, England: Cambridge University Press.

Krashen, S.
1982   *Principles and Practice in Second Language Acquisition.* Oxford: Pergamon.

Krashen, S., R. Scarcella, and M. Long, eds.
  1982 *Child-Adult Differences in Second Language Acquisition.* Rowley, MA: Newbury House.
Lambert, W.E.
  1975 Culture and language as factors in learning and education. Pp. 55-83 in A. Wolfgang, ed., *Education of Immigrant Students.* Toronto: Ontario Institute for Studies in Education.
Larsen-Freeman, D., and M. Long
  1990 *An Introduction to Second Language Acquisition Research.* London, England, and New York: Longman.
Leopold, W.
  1939 *Speech Development of a Bilingual Child: A Linguist's Record. Vol. 1: Vocabulary Growth in the First Two Years.* Evanston, IL: Northwestern University.
  1947 *Speech Development of a Bilingual Child: A Linguist's Record. Vol. 2: Sound Learning in the First Two Years.* Evanston, IL: Northwestern University.
  1949a *Speech Development of a Bilingual Child: A Linguist's Record. Vol. 3: Grammar and General Problems in the First Two Years.* Evanston, IL: Northwestern University.
  1949b *Speech Development of a Bilingual Child: A Linguist's Record. Vol. 4: Diary From Age Two.* Evanston, IL: Northwestern University.
Lieberson, S., G. Dalto, and M. Johnston
  1975 The course of mother-tongue diversity in nations. *American Journal of Sociology* 81:34-61.
Long, M.H.
  1983 Linguistic and conversational adjustments to non-native speakers. *Studies in Second Language Acquisition* 5(2):177-193.
  1990 The least a second language acquisition theory needs to explain. *TESOL Quarterly* 24(4):649-666.
Lopez, D.E.
  1978 Chicano language loyalty in an urban setting. *Sociology and Social Research* 62:267-278.
McLaughlin, B.
  1984 *Second-language Acquisition in Childhood: Volume 1, Preschool Children.* Hillsdale, NJ: Erlbaum.
  1985 *Second-language Acquisition in Childhood: Volume 2, Schoolage Children.* Hillsdale, NJ: Erlbaum.
Milk, R.
  1990 Preparing ESL and bilingual teachers for changing roles: Immersion for teachers of LEP children. *TESOL Quarterly* 24(3):407-426.
Odlin, T.
  1989 *Language Transfer: Cross-linguistic Influence in Language Learning.* Cambridge: Cambridge University Press.
Oller, J.W., Jr.
  1981 Language as intelligence. *Language Learning* 31:465-492.

Paul, B., and C. Jarvis
    1992   The effects of native language use in New York City pre-kindergarten classes. Paper presented at the 1992 Annual Meeting of the American Educational Research Association, San Francisco, CA. ERIC Document ED351874.

Peal, E., and W.E. Lambert
    1962   The relation of bilingualism to intelligence. *Psychological Monographs: General and Applied* 76(546):1-23.

Pearson, B., S. Fernández, V. Lewedeg, and D. Oller
    1997   The relation of input factors to lexical learning by bilingual infants (ages 8 to 30 months). *Applied Psycholinguistics* 18(1):41-62.

Pica, T.
    1987   Second-language acquisition, social interaction, and the classroom. *Applied Linguistics* 8(1):3-21.

Ramirez, D.J., S.D. Yuen, D.R. Ramey, and D.J. Pasta
    1991   *Final Report: National Longitudinal Study of Structured-English Immersion Strategy, Early-Exit and Late-Exit Transitional Bilingual Education Programs for Language-Minority Children. Volumes I and II.* San Mateo, CA: Aguirre International.

Reynolds, A.
    1991   *Bilingualism, Multiculturalism, and Second Language Learning.* Hillsdale, NJ: Erlbaum.

Romaine, J.
    1995   *Bilingualism.* 2nd ed. Oxford, England: Blackwell.

Ronjat, J.
    1913   *Le développement du langage observé chez un enfant bilingue.* Paris: Champion.

Seliger, H., and R. Vago, eds.
    1991   *First Language Attrition: Structural and Theoretical Perspectives.* Cambridge and New York: Cambridge University Press.

Shultz, N.W., Jr.
    1975   *On the autonomy and comparability of linguistic and ethnographic description.* Lisse, Netherlands: Peter de Ridder.

Snow, C.E.
    1987   Relevance of the notion of a critical period to language acquisition. Pp. 183-209 in M. Bornstein, ed., *Sensitive Periods in Development.* Hillsdale, NJ: Erlbaum.

van Lier, L.
    1988   *The Classroom and the Language Learner.* London, England: Longman.

Veltman, C.
    1983   *Language Shift in the United States.* New York: Mouton.

Weinreich, U.
    1953   *Languages in Contact.* The Hague: Mouton.

CHAPTER 3
COGNITIVE ASPECTS OF SCHOOL LEARNING:
LITERACY DEVELOPMENT AND CONTENT LEARNING

Adams, M.J.
  1990   *Beginning to Read: Thinking and Learning about Print.* Cambridge, MA: MIT Press.
Adams, M., and M. Bruck
  1995   Resolving the "great debate." *American Educator* 19(2):10-20.
Anderson, R.C., and P.D. Pearson
  1984   A schema-theoretic view of basic processes in reading. Pp. 255-291 in P. D. Pearson, ed., *Handbook of Reading Research.* New York: Longman.
Anderson, V., and M. Roit
  1996   Linking reading comprehension instruction to language development for language minority students. *Elementary School Journal* 96(3):295-310.
Barnett, M.A.
  1989   *More Than Meets the Eye: Foreign Language Reading. Language and Education: Theory and Practice.* Englewood Cliffs, NJ: ERIC.
Bereiter, C.
  1984   The limitations of interpretation (review of writing and the writer). *Curriculum Inquiry* 4:211-216.
Bereiter, C., and M. Bird
  1985   Use of thinking aloud in identification and teaching of reading comprehension strategies. *Cognition and Instruction* 2:131-156.
Bernhardt, E.B.
  1987   Cognitive processes in L2: An examination of reading behaviors. Pp. 35-50 in J. Lantolf and A. Labarca, eds., *Research in Second Language Learning: Focus on the Classroom.* Norwood, NJ: Ablex.
Bialystok, E., and K. Hakuta
  1994   *In Other Words.* New York: Basic Books.
Brown, A. L.
  1980   Metacognitive development and reading. Pp. 453-481 in R.J. Spiro, B.C. Bruce, and W.F. Brewer, eds., *Theoretical Issues in Reading Comprehension.* Hillsdale, NJ: Erlbaum.
Brown, A.L., J.D. Bransford, R.A. Ferrara, and J.C. Campione
  1983   Learning, remembering, and understanding. Pp. 77-166 in J.H. Flavell and E.M. Markman, eds., Handbook of Child Psychology: Vol 3. *Cognitive Development.* 4th ed. New York: Wiley.
Carrell, P.L.
  1987   Content and formal schemata in ESL reading. *TESOL Quarterly* 21(3):461-481.
Casanave, C.P.
  1988   Comprehension monitoring in ESL reading: A neglected essential. *TESOL Quarterly* 22:283-302.
Chall, J. S.
  1967   *Learning to Read: The Great Debate.* New York: McGraw-Hill.
  1983   *Stages of Reading Development.* New York: McGraw-Hill.

Chi, M.T.H., R. Glaser, and E. Rees
  1982 Expertise in problem solving. Pp. 7-75 in R.J. Sternberg, ed., *Advances in the Psychology of Human Intelligence, Vol 1.* Hillsdale, NJ: Erlbaum.
Chi, M.T.H,, and R. Koeske
  1983 Network representation of a child's dinosaur knowledge. *Development Psychology* 19:29-39.
Chi, M.T.H., and S. Ceci
  1987 Content knowledge: Its role, representation, and restructuring in memory development. Pp. 91-142 in H.W. Reese, ed., *Advances in Child Development and Behavior, Vol. 20.* New York: Academic Press.
Christian, D.
  1996 Language development in two-way immersion: Trends and prospects. In James E. Alatis, Carolyn A. Straehle, Maggie Ronkin, and Brent Gallenberger, eds., *Georgetown University Round Table 1996.* Washington, DC: Georgetown University Press.
Cohen, E.G.
  1990 Teaching in multiculturally heterogeneous classrooms: Findings from a model program. *McGill Journal of Education* 26(1):7-23.
Collier, V.P., and W.P. Thomas
  1989 How quickly can immigrants become proficient in school English? *Journal of Educational Issues of Language Minority Students* 5:26-38.
Cummins, J.
  1991 Language development and academic learning. Pp. 161-175 in L.M. Malavé and G. Duquette, eds., *Language, Culture and Cognition.* Clevedon, England: Multilingual Matters.
Devine, J.
  1987 General language competence and adult second language reading. Pp. 73-86 in J. Devine, P. Carrell, and D. Eskey, eds., *Research in Reading English as a Second Language.* Washington, DC: Teachers of English to Speakers of Other Languages.
Diaz, R.M.
  1986 Bilingual cognitive development: Addressing three gaps in current research. *Child Development* 56:1376-1388.
Elley, W.B.
  1981 A comparison of content-interest and structuralist reading programs in Niue primary schools. *New Zealand Journal of Educational Studies* 15(1):39-53.
Feitelson, D.
  1988 *Facts and Fads in Beginning Reading: A Cross-Language Perspective.* Norwood, NJ: Ablex.
Fitzgerald, J.
  1995 English-as-a-second-language learners' cognitive reading processes: A review of research in the United States. *Review of Educational Research* 65:145-190.
Flesch, R.F.
  1955 *Why Johnny Can't Read.* New York: Harper Row.
Gersten, R.
  1996 Literacy instruction for language-minority students: The transition years. *The Elementary School Journal* 96(3):228-244.

Hakuta, K., and R.M. Diaz
  1985 The relationship between degree of bilingualism and cognitive ability: A critical discussion and some new longitudinal data. Pp. 319-345 in K. Nelson, ed., *Children's Language*. 5th ed. Hillsdale, NJ: Erlbaum.
Heibert, J.
  1986 *Conceptual and Procedural Knowledge: The Case of Mathematics*. Hillsdale, NJ: Erlbaum.
Johnson, P.
  1981 Effects on reading comprehension of language complexity and cultural background of a text. *TESOL Quarterly* 15:169-181.
Kintsch, W., and T.A. van Dijk
  1978 Toward a model of text comprehension and production. *Psychological Review* 85(5):363-394.
Klingner, J.K., and S. Vaughn
  1996 Reciprocal teaching of reading comprehension strategies for students with learning disabilities who use English as a second language. *The Elementary School Journal* 96(3):275-294.
Lampert, M.
  1986 Knowing, doing, and teaching multiplication. *Cognition and Instruction* 4(4):303-342.
McKeown, M., I. Beck, G.M. Sinatra, and J.A. Loxterman
  1992 The contribution of prior knowledge and coherent text to comprehension. *Reading Research Quarterly* 27:79-93.
Palincsar, A.S., and A.L. Brown
  1984 Reciprocal teaching of comprehension-fostering and comprehension-monitoring activities. *Cognition and Instruction* 1(2):117-175.
Peal, E., and W.E. Lambert
  1962 The relation of bilingualism to intelligence. *Psychological Monographs: General and Applied* 76(546):1-23.
Pearson, D.P., J. Hansen, and C. Gordon
  1979 The effect of background knowledge on young children's comprehension of explicit and implicit information. *Journal of,Reading Behavior* 11(3):201-209.
Purcell-Gates, V.
  1996 Process teaching with explicit explanation and feedback in a university-based clinic. In E. McIntyre and M. Pressley, eds., *Balanced Instruction: Strategies and Skills in Whole Language*. Norwood, MA: Christopher-Gordon.
Rayner, K., and A. Pollatsek
  1989 *The Psychology of Reading*. Englewood Cliffs, NJ: Prentice Hall.
Schwab, J.J.
  1978 Education and the structure of the disciplines. In I. Westbury and N.J. Wilkof, eds., *Science, Curriculum, and Liberal Education: Selected Essays*. Chicago: University of Chicago Press.
Scribner, S.
  1984 Studying work intelligence. Pp. 9-40 in B. Rogoff and J. Lave, eds., *Everyday Cognition: Its Development in Social Context*. Cambridge, MA: Harvard University Press.

Skutnabb-Kangas, T.
    1979 *Language in the Process of Cultural Assimilation and Structural Incorporation
          of Linguistic Minorities.* Arlington, VA: National Clearinghouse for Bilingual
          Education.
Slavin, R., and R. Yampolsky
    1992 *Success for All. Effects on Students with Limited English Proficiency: A Three-
          year Evaluation.* Report No. 29. Baltimore, MD: Center for Research on
          Effective Schooling for Disadvantaged Students, The Johns Hopkins Univer-
          sity.
Stodolsky, S.
    1988 *The Subject Matters: Classroom Activity in Mathematics and Social Studies.*
          Chicago: University of Chicago Press.
Wong Fillmore, L., and C. Valadez
    1986 Teaching bilingual learners. Pp. 648-685 in M.C. Wittrock, ed., *Handbook of
          Research on Teaching.* 3rd ed. New York: Macmillan.

CHAPTER 4
THE SOCIAL CONTEXT OF SCHOOL LEARNING

Allexsaht-Snider, M.
    1992 Bilingual parents perspectives on home-school linkages. Paper presented at the
          annual meeting of the American Educational Research Association, April 20-
          24, San Francisco, CA.
Au, K.H.P.
    1980 Participation structures in a reading lesson with Hawaiian children: Analysis of
          a culturally appropriate instructional event. *Anthropology and Education Quar-
          terly* 11(2):91-115.
Au, K.H.P., and J.M. Mason
    1981 Social organizational factors in learning to read: The balance of rights hypoth-
          esis. *Reading Research Quarterly* 17(1):115-152.
Bempechat, J., N. Jiminez, and S. Graham
    1996 Motivational and cultural factors in learning: Implications for poor and minor-
          ity children, youth and families. *Journal of Child and Youth Care Work 11.*
Boggs, S.
    1985 *Speaking, Relating, and Learning: A Study of Hawaiian Children at Home and
          School.* Norwood, NJ: Ablex.
Choi, E., J. Bempechat, and H. Ginsburg
    1994 Educational socialization in Korean-American children: A longitudinal study.
          Journal of Applied Developmental Psychology 15:313-318.
Cohen, E.G.
    1984a Talking and working together: Status, interaction, and learning. Pp. 171-186 in
          P. Peterson, L. C. Wilkinson, and M. Hallinan, eds., *The Social Context of
          Instruction.* New York: Academic Press.
    1984b The desegregated school: Problems in status power and interethnic climate.
          Pp. 77-96 in N. Miller and M. B. Brewer, eds., *Groups in Contact: The Psy-
          chology of Desegregation.* New York: Academic Press.

1994 *Designing Groupwork: Strategies for the Heterogeneous Classroom, 2nd ed.* New York: Teachers College Press.

Cohen, E.G., and R.A. Lotan

1995 Producing equal-status interaction in the heterogeneous classroom. *American Educational Research Journal* 32:99-120.

Cohen, E.G., and S.S. Roper

1972 Modification of interracial interaction disability: An application of status characteristic theory. *American Sociological Review* 37:643-657.

Comer, J.P.

1986 Parent participation in the schools. *Phi Delta Kappan* 67(6):442-446.

Dalton, S., and J. Sison

1995 *Enacting Instructional Conversation with Spanish-speaking Students in Middle School Mathematics.* Educational Research Report No. 12. Santa Cruz, CA, and Washington, DC: National Center for Research on Cultural Diversity and Second Language Learning.

Dauber, S.L., and J.L. Epstein

1993 Parents' attitudes and practices of involvement in inner-city elementary and middle schools. Pp. 53-71 in N. Chavkin, ed., *Families and Schools in a Pluralistic Society.* Albany, NY: SUNY Press.

Delgado-Gaitan, C.

1990 *Literacy for Empowerment: The Role of Parents in Children's Education.* New York: Falmer Press.

DeVos, G.

1978 Selective permeability and reference group sanctioning: Psychological continuities in role degradation. Pp. 7-24 in Y. Yinger and S. Cutler, eds., *Competing Models of Multiethnic and Multiracial Societies.* New York: American Sociological Association.

Diaz-Soto, L.

1988 The home environment of higher and lower achieving Puerto Rican children. *Hispanic Journal of Behavioral Sciences* 10(2):161-168.

Dornbusch, S.M., and P.L. Ritter

1988 Parents of high school students: A neglected resource. *Educational Horizons* 66:75-77.

Epstein, J., and S. Dauber

1991 School programs and teacher practices of parental involvement in inner-city elementary and middle schools. *Elementary School Journal* 91(3):289-303.

Epstein, J., T.L. Connors, and K. Salinas

1995 Five-Year Review: Research on Families, Communities, Schools, and Children's Learning. Paper presented at the annual meeting of the American Educational Research Association, San Francisco, CA.

Garcia, E.E.

1993 Language, culture, and education. Pp. 51-98 in L. Darling-Hammond, ed., *Review of Research in Education.* Vol. 19. Washington, DC: American Educational Research Association.

Gee, J.P.

  1988a Discourse systems and aspirin bottles: On literacy. *Journal of Education* 170(1):27-40.

  1988b Dracula, the vampire lestat, and TESOL. *TESOL Quarterly* 22(2):201-225.

Gibson, M.A.

  1988 *Accommodation Without Assimilation: Sikh Immigrants in an American High School.* Ithaca: Cornell University Press.

Giles, M.W.

  1977 Percent black and racial hostility: An old assumption reexamined. *Social Science Quarterly* 58(3):412-417.

Gimmestad, B.J., and E. DeChiara

  1982 Dramatic plays: A vehicle for prejudice reduction in the elementary school. *Journal of Educational Research* 76(1):45-49.

Goldenberg, C., and R. Gallimore

  1991 Local knowledge, research knowledge, and educational change: A case study of first-grade Spanish reading improvement. *Educational Researcher* 20(8):2-14.

Gutierrez, K.D.

  1992 A comparison of instructional contexts in writing process classrooms with Latino children. *Education and Urban Society* 24(2):244-262.

  1994 Language borders: Recitation as hegemonic discourse. *International Journal of Educational Reform* 3(1):22-36.

Harklau, L.

  1994 Tracking and linguistic minority students: Consequences of ability grouping for second language learners. *Linguistics and Education* 6(3):217-244.

Heath, S.B.

  1983 *Ways with Words: Language, Life, and Work in Communities and Classrooms.* New York: Cambridge University Press.

Henderson, A.

  1987 *The Evidence Continues to Grow: Parent Involvement Improves Student Achievement.* Columbia, MD: National Committee for Citizens in Education.

Hidalgo, N.M., J. Bright, S.F. Sui, S. Swap, and J. Epstein

  1995 Research on families, schools, and communities: A multicultural perspective. Pp. 498-524 in J. A. Banks and C.A. Banks, eds., *Handbook of Research on Multicultural Education* (Chapter 28). New York: Macmillan.

Isaacs, H.R.

  1992 Language as a factor in inter-group conflict. Pp. 466-478 in J. Crawford, ed., *Language Loyalties: A Source Book on the Official English Controversy.* Chicago: University of Chicago Press.

Johnson, V.R.

  1993 *Parent/Family Centers in Schools: Expanding Outreach and Promoting Collaboration.* Center Report 20. Baltimore, MD: Center on Families Communities Schools and Children's Learning.

  1994 *Parent Centers in Urban Schools: Four Case Studies.* (Center Report 23.) Baltimore: Center on Families Communities Schools and Children's Learning.

Lambert, W., and M. Cazabon
   1994   *Students' Views of the Amigos Program. Research Report #11.* Santa Cruz, CA, and Washington, DC: National Center for Research on Cultural Diversity and Second Language Learning.
Linguistics and Education
   1994   *Linguistics and Education* 5 (whole issue).
Matsuda, M.
   1989   Working with Asian parents: Some communication strategies. *Topics in Language Disorders* 45-53.
McCollum, P.
   1993   Learning to Value English: Cultural Capital in a Two-Way Bilingual Program. Paper presented at the AERA annual meeting, Atlanta, GA.
McGregor, J.
   1993   Effectiveness of role playing and antiracist teaching in reducing student prejudice. *Journal of Educational Research* 86(4):215-226.
Michaels, S.
   1991   Sharing time. *Language in Society* 10:423-447.
Moll, L.C., and S. Diaz
   1987   Changes as the goal of educational research. *Anthropology and Education Quarterly* 18:300-311.
Ogbu, J.U.
   1978   *Minority Education and Caste: The American System in Cross-Cultural Perspective.* New York: Academic Press.
   1995   Understanding cultural diversity and learning. Pp. 582-593 in J.A. Banks and C.A.M. Banks, eds., *Handbook of Research on Multicultural Education.* New York: Macmillan.
Ogbu, J.U., and M.E. Matute-Bianchi
   1986   Understanding sociocultural factors: Knowledge, identity, and school adjustment. Pp. 73-142 in *Beyond Language: Social and Cultural Factors in Schooling Language Minority Students.* Los Angeles: Evaluation, Dissemination, and Assessment Center, California State University.
Patthey-Chavez, G., and C. Goldenberg
   1995   Changing instructional discourse for changing students: The instructional conversation. Pp. 205-230 in R. Macías and R. García Ramos, eds., *Changing Schools for Changing Students: An Anthology of Research on Language Minorities, Schools and Society.* Santa Barbara, CA: University of California Linguistic Minority Research Institute.
Philips, S.U.
   1983   *The Invisible Culture: Communication in Classroom and Community on the Warm Springs Reservation Indian Reservation.* New York: Longman.
Robledo Montecel, M.
   1993   *Hispanic Families as Valued Partners: An Educator's Guide.* San Antonio, TX: Intercultural Development Research Association.
Rubio, O.
   1995   'Yo soy voluntaria:' Volunteering in a dual-language school. *Urban Education* 29(4):396-409.

Rueda, R., C. Goldenberg, and R. Gallimore
  1992   *Rating Instructional Conversations: A Guide.* Educational Practice Report,
          No. 4. Washington, DC: Center for Applied Linguistics.
Ryan, E.B., and M.A. Carranza
  1977   Ingroup and outgroup reactions to Mexican American language varieties. Pp.
          59-82 in H. Giles, ed., *Language, Ethnicity and Intergroup Relations.* New
          York: Academic Press.
Saunders, W., C. Goldenberg, and J. Hamann
  1992   Instructional conversations beget instructional conversations. *Teaching and
          Teacher Education* 8:199-218.
Slavin, R.E.
  1985   Cooperative learning: Applying contact theory in desegregated schools. *Jour-
          nal of Social Issues* 41:45-62.
  1995   Cooperative learning and intergroup relations. Pp. 628-634 in J.A. Banks and
          C.A.M. Banks, eds., *Handbook of Research on Multicultural Education.* New
          York: Macmillan.
Smith, C.
  1993   Parents and teachers in partnership. *Gifted Child Today* Nov/Dec:16-19.
Stevenson, H.W., S.Y. Lee, and J.W. Stigler
  1986   Mathematics achievement of Chinese, Japanese, and American children. *Sci-
          ence* 231:693-699.
Stevenson, H.W., C. Chen, and D.H. Uttal
  1990   Beliefs and achievement: A study of black, white, and Hispanic children. *Child
          Development* 61(2):508-523.
Suarez-Orozco, C., and M. Suarez-Orozco
  1995   *Transformations: Migration, Family Life, and Achievement Motivation Among
          Latino and White Adolescents.* Stanford, CA: Stanford University Press.
Tuan, M.
  1995   Korean and Russian students in a Los Angeles high school: Exploring the
          alternative strategies of two high-achieving groups. In Ruben G. Rumbaut and
          Wayne A. Cornelius, eds., *California's Immigrant Children: Theory, Research,
          and Implications for Educational Policy.* University of California, San Diego:
          Center for U.S.-American Studies.

CHAPTER 5
STUDENT ASSESSMENT

Abedi, J., C. Lord, and J. Plummer
  1995   *Language Background Report.* Graduate School of Education, National Center
          for Research on Evaluation, Standards, and Student Testing. Los Angeles:
          University of California at Los Angeles.
Alderman, D.
  1981   Language proficiency as a moderator variable in testing academic aptitude.
          Journal of Educational Psychology 74:580-587.

American Educational Research Association, American Psychological Association, and
National Council on Measurement in Education
   1985   *Standards of Educational and Psychological Testing.* Washington, DC: American Psychological Association.
August, D., and J. Lara
   1996   *Systemic Reform and Limited English Proficient Students.* Washington, DC: Council of Chief State School Officers.
August, D., K. Hakuta, F. Olguin, and D. Pompa
   1995   *LEP Students and Title I: A Guidebook for Educators.* Washington, DC: National Clearinghouse for Bilingual Education.
Carroll, J.B.
   1958   Communication theory, linguistics, and psycholinguistics. *Review of Educational Research* 28(2):79-88.
Cheung, O.M., and L.W. Soloman
   1991   *Summary of State Practices Concerning the Assessment of and the Data Collection about Limited English Proficient (LEP) Students.* Washington, DC: Council of Chief State School Officers.
Cloud, N.
   1991   Educational assessment. Pp. 219-245 in E.V. Hamayan and J.S. Damico, eds., *Limiting Bias in the Assessment of Bilingual Students.* Austin, TX: Pro-Ed.
Durán, R.P.
   1989   Assessment and instruction of at-risk Hispanic students. *Exceptional Children* 56(2):154-158.
Feurerstein, R.
   1979   *The Dynamic Assessment of Retarded Persons.* Baltimore, MD: University Park Press.
Garcia, G.E.
   1991   Factors influencing the English reading test performance of Spanish-speaking Hispanic children. *Research Reading Quarterly* 26(4):371-392.
Garcia, G.E., and P.D. Pearson
   1994   Assessment and diversity. *Review of Research in Education* (20):337-391.
Genesee, F., and E.V. Hamayan
   1994   Classroom-based assessment. In F. Genesee, ed., *Educating Second Language Children: The Whole Child, the Whole Curriculum, the Whole Community.* New York: Cambridge University Press.
Hafner, A.
   1995   Assessment Practices: Developing and Modifying Statewide Assessments for LEP Students. Paper presented at the annual conference on Large Scale Assessment sponsored by the Council of Chief State School Officers, June 1995. School of Education, California State University, Los Angeles.
Hambleton, R.K., and A. Kanjee
   1994   Enhancing the validity of cross-cultural studies: Improvements in instrument translation methods. In T. Husen and T.N. Postlewaite, eds., *International Encyclopedia of Education* (2nd edition). Oxford, UK: Pergamon Press.
Leinhardt, G.
   1978   Educational opportunity: Opportunity to learn. Pp. 15-24, Chapter III in *Perspectives in the Instructional Dimensions Study: A Supplemental Report from*

the National Institute of Education. Washington, DC: National Institute of Education.

Lewis, J.
1991   Innovative approaches in assessment. In R.J. Samuda and S.L. Kong, J. Cummins, J. Pascual-Leone, and J. Lewis, eds., *Assessment and Placement of Minority Students.* Toronto, Canada: C.J. Hogrefe.

Lindholm, K.
1994   Standardized Achievement Tests vs. Alternative Assessment: Are Results Complementary or Contradictory? Paper presented at the American Educational Research Association, New Orleans, April.

McLaughlin, B.
1984   *Second-Language Acquisition in Childhood,* 2d ed. Hillsdale, NJ: Erlbaum.

McLaughlin, B., A. Blanchard, and Y. Osanai
1995   *Assessing Language Development in Bilingual Preschool Children.* NCBE Program Information Guide Series, No. 22. Washington, DC: National Clearinghouse for Bilingual Education.

Meisels, S.
1994   Designing meaningful measurements for early childhood. Pp. 202-222 in B. Mallory and R. New, eds., *Diversity and Developmentally Appropriate Practices: Challenges for Early Childhood Education.* New York: Teachers College Press.

Messick, C.K.
1988   Ins and outs of the acquisition of spatial terms. *Topics in Language Disorders* 8(2):14-25.

Navarette, C., J. Wilde, C. Nelson, R. Martinez, and G. Hargett
1990   *Informal Assessment in Educational Evaluation: Implications for Bilingual Education Programs.* Program Information Guide No. 13. Washington, DC: National Clearinghouse for Bilingual Education.

Rivera, C.
1984   *Communicative Competence Approaches to Language Proficiency Assessment: Research and Application.* Multilingual Matters 9. Rosslyn, VA: InterAmerican Research Associates.
1995   *How We Can Ensure Equity in Statewide Assessment Programs?* Findings from a national survey of assessment directors on statewide assessment policies for LEP students, presented at annual meeting of the National Conference on Large Scale Assessment, June 18, 1995, Phoenix, AZ. The Evaluation Assistance Center East. Washington, DC: George Washington University Institute for Equity and Excellence in Education.

Saville-Troike, M.
1991   *Teaching and Testing for Academic Achievement: The Role of Language Development.* Focus, Occasional Papers in Bilingual Education, No. 4. Washington, DC: National Clearinghouse for Bilingual Education.

Short, D.
1991   *How to Integrate Language and Content Instruction: A Training Manual.* Washington, DC: Center for Applied Linguistics.

Teachers of English to Speakers of Other Languages, Inc.
  1997   ESL Standards for Pre-K - 12 Students. Alexandria, VA: Teachers of English
         to Speakers of Other Languages, Inc.
Valdez Pierce, L., and J.M. O'Malley
  1992   *Performance and Portfolio Assessment for Language Minority Students.* NCBE
         Program Information Guide Series. Washington, DC: National Clearinghouse
         for Bilingual Education.
Wong Fillmore, L.
  1982   Language minority students and school participation: What kind of English is
         needed? *Journal of Education* 164:143-156.
Wong Fillmore, L., and J. Lara
  1996   *Summary of the Proposal Setting the Pace for English Learning: Focus on
         Assessment Tools and Staff Development.* Washington, DC: Council of Chief
         State School Officers.

CHAPTER 6
PROGRAM EVALUATION

Baker, K.A., and A.A. de Kanter
  1981   *Effectiveness of Bilingual Education: A Review of the Literature.* Washington,
         DC: U.S. Department of Education.
Bryk, A.S., and S.W. Raudenbush
  1992   *Hierarchical Linear Models: Applications and Data Analysis Methods.*
         Newbury Park, CA: Sage.
Burkheimer, Jr., G.J., A.J. Conger, G.H. Dunteman, B.G. Elliott, and K.A. Mowbray
  1989   *Effectiveness of Services for Language-minority Limited-English-proficient Stu-
         dents.* 2 vols. Technical Report. Research Triangle Park, NC: Research Tri-
         angle Institute.
Campbell, D.T., and J.C. Stanley
  1963   Experimental and quasi-experimental designs for research in teaching. In N.L.
         Gage, ed., *Handbook of Research on Teaching.* Chicago: Rand-McNally.
Cousins, J.B., and L.M. Earl
  1992   The case for participatory evaluation. *Educational Evaluation and Policy
         Analysis* 14:397-418.
Crawford, J.
  1995   *Bilingual Education: History, Politics, Theory, and Practice.* Los Angeles:
         Bilingual Educational Services.
Dannoff, M.N.
  1978   *Evaluation of the Impact of ESEA Title VII Spanish-English Bilingual Educa-
         tion Programs.* Technical Report. Washington, DC: American Institutes for
         Research.
Development Associates
  1984   *Overview of the Research Design Plans for the National Longitudinal Study of
         the Effectiveness of Services for Language Minority Students.* Arlington, VA:
         Development Associates.

Fetterman, D.M., S.J. Kaftarian, and A. Wandersman, eds.
1995   *Empowerment Evaluation: Knowledge and Tools for Self-Assessment and Accountability.* Thousand Oaks, CA: Sage.
Gersten, R.
1985   Structured immersion for language minority students: Results of a longitudinal evaluation. *Education Evaluation and Policy Analysis* 7(3):187-196.
Gersten, R., and J. Woodward
1995   A longitudinal study of transitional and immersion bilingual education programs in one district. *Elementary School Journal* 95(3):223-239.
Gersten, R., R. Taylor, J. Woodward, and W.A.T. White
1984   *Structured English Immersion for Hispanic Students in the U.S.: Findings from the Fourteen-year Evaluation of the Uvalde, Texas, Program.* Technical Report 84-1, Follow Through Project. Eugene: University of Oregon.
Ginsburg, A.L.
1992   Improving bilingual education programs through evaluation. Pp. 31-42 in *Proceedings of the Second National Research Symposium on Limited English Proficient Student Issues: Focus on Evaluation and Measurement.* Vol. 1. OBEMLA. Washington, DC: U.S. Department of Education.
Gold, T., and F. Tempes
1987   A State Agency Partnership with Schools to Improve Bilingual Education. Paper presented at the annual meeting of the American Educational Research Association, Washington, DC. California State Department of Education.
Lam, T.C.M.
1992   Review of practices and problems in the evaluation of bilingual education. *Review of Educational Research* 62(2):181-203.
Lord, F.M.
1967   A paradox in the interpretation of group comparisons. *Psychological Bulletin* 68:304-305.
Meyer, M.M., and S.E. Fienberg, eds.
1992   *Assessing Evaluation Studies: The Case of Bilingual Education Strategies.* Panel to Review Evaluation Studies of Bilingual Education, Committee on National Statistics, National Research Council. Washington, DC: National Academy Press.
Ramirez, D.J., S.D. Yuen, D.R. Ramey, and D.J. Pasta
1991   *Final Report: National Longitudinal Study of Structured-English Immersion Strategy, Early-Exit and Late-Exit Transitional Bilingual Education Programs for Language-Minority Children, Vol. 1 and 11, Technical Report.* San Mateo, CA: Aguirre International.
Rossell, C.H., and K. Baker
1996   The educational effectiveness of bilingual education. *Research in the Teaching of English* 30(1):7-74.
Rossell, C.H., and J.M. Ross
1986   The social science evidence on bilingual education. *Journal of Law and Education* 15(4):385-419.
Samaniego, F., and L. Eubank
1991   *A Statistical Analysis of California's Case Study Project in Bilingual Education.* TR #208. Intercollegiate Division of Statistics. Davis: University of California.

Thomas, W., and V. Collier
   1995   *Language Minority Student Achievement and Program Effectiveness.* Washington, DC: National Clearinghouse for Bilingual Education.
U.S. Department of Education
   1991   *The Condition of Bilingual Education in the Nation: A Report to the Congress and the President.* Office of the Secretary. Washington, DC: U.S. Department of Education, Washington, DC.
U.S. General Accounting Office
   1987   Bilingual Education: A New Look at the Research Evidence. Briefing report to the Chairman, Committee on Education, Labor, House of Representatives, GAO/PEMD-87-12BR. Washington, DC.
Willig, A.C.
   1985   A meta-analysis of selected studies on the effectiveness of bilingual education. *Review of Educational Research* 55(3):269-317.

CHAPTER 7
STUDIES OF SCHOOL AND CLASSROOM EFFECTIVENESS

Anderson, R., R. St. Pierre, E. Proper, and L. Stebbins
   1978   Pardon us, but what was the question again? A response to the critique of the follow-through evaluation. *Harvard Educational Review* 48:161-170.
Berman, P., J. Chambers, P. Gandara, B. McLaughlin, C. Minicucci, B. Nelson, L. Olsen, and T. Parrish
   1992   *Meeting the challenge of language diversity: An evaluation of programs for pupils with limited proficiency in English.* Vol. 1 [R-119/1: Executive Summary; Vol. 2 [R-119/2]: Findings and Conclusions; Vol. 3 [R-119/3]: Case Study Appendix. Berkeley, CA: BW Associates.
Berman, P., B. McLaughlin, B. McLeod, C. Minicucci, B. Nelson, and K. Woodworth
   1995   School Reform and Student Diversity: Case Studies of Exemplary Practices for LEP Students (Draft Report). National Center for Research on Cultural Diversity and Second Language Learning and BW Associates. Berkeley, CA.
Calderon, M., R. Hertz-Lazarowitz, and R. Slavin
   1996   Effects of Bilingual Cooperative Integrated Reading and Composition on Students Transitioning from Spanish to English Reading. Unpublished paper for the Office of Educational Research and Improvement, U.S. Department of Education, Washington, DC.
Carter, T., and M. Chatfield
   1986   Effective bilingual schools: Implications for policy and practice. *American Journal of Education* 95:200-232.
Chamot, A.U., M. Dale, J.M. O'Malley, and G. Spanos
   1992   Learning and problem solving strategies of ESL students. *Bilingual Research Journal* 16(3-4):1-33.
Cohen, E.
   1984   Talking and working together: Status, interaction, and learning. Pp. 171-187, Chapter 10 in P.L. Peterson et al., eds., *The Social Context of Instruction: Group Organization and Group Processes.* Orlando, FL: Academic Press.

Dianda, M., and J. Flaherty

1995 *Effects of Success for All on the Reading Achievement of First Graders in California Bilingual Programs.* Los Alamitos, CA: The Southwest Regional Educational Laboratory.

Edelsky, C., K. Draper, and K. Smith

1983 Hookin' 'em in at the start of school in a 'whole language' classroom. *Anthropology & Education Quarterly* 14:257-281.

Garcia, E.E.

1990a Instructional discourse in "effective" Hispanic classrooms. Pp. 104-117 in Rodolfo Jacobson and Christian Faltis, eds., *Language Distribution Issues in Bilingual Schooling.* Bristol, PA: Multilingual Matters.

1990b Education of Linguistically and Culturally Diverse Students: Effective Instructional Practices. The National Center for Research on Cultural Diversity and Second Language Learning. Educational Practice Report, No. 1. Center for Applied Linguistics, Washington, D.C.

Gersten, R.

1996 Literacy instruction for language-minority students: The transition years. *The Elementary School Journal* 96(3):228-244.

Gold, N., and F. Tempes

1987 A State Agency Partnership with Schools to Improve Bilingual Education. Paper presented at the annual meeting of the American Educational Research Association, Washington, DC. California State Department of Education.

Goldenberg, C.

1993 The home-school connection in bilingual education. Pp. 225-250 in B. Arias and U. Casanova, eds., *Ninety-second Yearbook of the National Society for the Study of Education. Bilingual education: Politics, Research, and Practice.* Chicago, IL: University of Chicago Press.

Goldenberg, C., and R. Gallimore

1991 Local knowledge, research knowledge, and educational change: A case study of first-grade Spanish reading improvement. *Educational Researcher* 20(8):2-14.

Goldenberg, C., and J. Sullivan

1994 *Making Change Happen in a Language-minority School: A Search for Coherence.* EPR #13. Washington, DC: Center for Applied Linguistics.

Henderson, R.W., and E.M. Landesman

1992 *Mathematics and Middle School Students of Mexican Descent: The Effects of Thematically Integrated Instruction.* Research Report: 5. National Center for Research on Cultural Diversity and Second Language Learning, Santa Cruz: University of California.

Hernandez, J.S.

1991 Assisted performance in reading comprehension strategies with non-English proficient students. *The Journal of Educational Issues of Language Minority Students* 8:91-112.

Jussim, L.

1986 Self-fulfilling prophecies: A theoretical and integrative review. *Psychological Review* 93:429-445.

Krashen, S., and D. Biber
  1988 *On Course: Bilingual Education's Success in California.* Sacramento, CA: California Association for Bilingual Education.
Lucas, T., and A. Katz
  1994 Reframing the debate: The roles of native languages in English-only programs for language minority students. *TESOL Quarterly* 28(3):537-561.
Lucas, T., R. Henze, and R. Donato
  1990 Promoting the success of Latino language-minority students: An exploratory study of six high schools. *Harvard Educational Review* 60:315-340.
Mace-Matluck, B.J., W.A. Hoover, and R.C. Calfee
  1989 Teaching reading to bilingual children: A longitudinal study of teaching and learning in the early grades. *NABE Journal* 13:3.
Minicucci, C., and L. Olsen
  1992 An exploratory study of secondary LEP programs. R-119/5; Vol. V of *Meeting the Challenge of Language Diversity: An Evaluation of Programs for Pupils with Limited Proficiency in English.* Berkeley, CA: BW Associates.
Moll, L.C.
  1988 Some key issues in teaching Latino students. *Language Arts* 65(5):465-472.
Moll, L.C., C. Amanti, D. Neff, and N. Gonzalez
  1992 Funds of knowledge for teaching: Using a qualitative approach to connect homes and classrooms. *Theory into Practice* 31(2):132-141.
Muniz-Swicegood, M.
  1994 The effects of metacognitive reading strategy training on the reading performance and student reading analysis strategies of third-grade bilingual students. *Bilingual Research Journal* 18(1&2):83-97.
Pease-Alvarez, L., E.E. Garcia, and P. Espinosa
  1991 Effective instruction for language-minority students: An early childhood case study. *Early Childhood Research Quarterly* 6:347-361.
Rosebery, A.S., B. Warren, and F.R. Conant
  1992 Appropriating scientific discourse: Findings from language minority classrooms. *The Journal of the Learning Sciences* 2(1):61-94.
Rosenshine, B., and R. Stevens
  1986 Teaching Functions. Pp. 376-391 in M. Wittrock. ed., *Handbook of Research on Teaching.* 3rd ed. New York: Macmillan.
Samaniego, F., and L. Eubank
  1991 *A Statistical Analysis of California's Case Study Project in Bilingual Education* (TR#208). Davis, CA: Intercollegiate Division of Statistics, University of California, Davis.
Saunders, W., and C. Goldenberg
  In   Can you engage students in high-level talk about text and support literal com-
  press prehension too? The effects of instructional conversation on transition students' concepts of friendship and story comprehension. In R. Horowitz, ed., *Talk About Text: Developing Understanding of the World Through Talk and Text.* Newark, DE: International Reading Association.

Saunders, W., G. O'Brien, D. Lennon, and J. McLean
1996   Making the transition to English literacy successful: Effective strategies for studying literature with transition students. In R. Gersten and R. Jimenez, eds, *Effective Strategies for Teaching Language Minority Students*. Monterey, CA: Brooks Cole.

Short, D.J.
1994   Expanding middle school horizons: Integrating language, culture, and social studies. *TESOL Quarterly* 28(3):581-608.

Slavin, R., and N. Madden
1994   Lee Conmigo: Effects of Success for All in Bilingual First Grades. Paper presented at the annual meeting of the American Educational Research Association, New Orleans, April. Center for Children Placed at Risk of School Failure, Johns Hopkins University, Baltimore, Maryland.
1995   Effects of Success for All on the Achievement of English Language Learners. Paper presented at the annual meeting of the American Educational Research Association, San Francisco, April. Center for Children Placed at Risk of School Failure, Johns Hopkins University, Baltimore, Maryland.

Slavin, R., and R. Yampolsky
1992   *Success for All. Effects on Students with Limited English Proficiency: A Three-year Evaluation*. Report No. 29. Baltimore, MD: Center for Research on Effective Schooling for Disadvantaged Students, The Johns Hopkins University.

Sternberg, R.J.
1986   Cognition and instruction: Why the marriage sometimes ends in divorce. Pp 375-382 in R.F. Dillon and R.J. Sternberg, eds., *Cognition and Instruction*. Orlando, FL: Academic Press.

Tharp, R.G.
1982   The effective instruction of comprehension: Results and description of the Kamehameha Early Education Program. *Reading Research Quarterly* 17(4): 503-527.

Tikunoff, W.J.
1983   *An Emerging Description of Successful Bilingual Instruction: Executive Summary of Part I of the SBIF Study*. San Francisco, CA: Far West Laboratory for Educational Research and Development.

Tikunoff, W.J., B.A. Ward, L.D. van Broekhuizen, M. Romero, L.V. Castaneda, T. Lucas, and A. Katz
1991   *A Descriptive Study of Significant Features of Exemplary Special Alternative Instructional Programs*. Final Report and Vol. 2: Report for Practitioners. Los Alamitos, CA: The Southwest Regional Educational Laboratory.

Wong Fillmore, L., P. Ammon, B. McLaughlin, and M. Ammon
1985   *Learning English through Bilingual Instruction*. Final Report. Berkeley: University of California.

Biographical Sketches
of Committee Members and Staff

KENJI HAKUTA (*Chair*) is professor of education at Stanford University, where he teaches in the Program of Language, Literacy and Culture and the Program of Psychological Studies in Education. An experimental psychologist by training, his current research is on the linguistic development of bilingual children. His publications include *Mirror of Language: The Debate on Bilingualism* (Basic Books, 1986) and *In Other Words: The Science and Psychology of Second Language Acquisition* (Basic Books, 1994). He serves as cochair of the National Educational Policy and Priorities Board for the U.S. Department of Education. Dr. Hakuta has a Ph.D. in experimental psychology from Harvard University.

DIANE AUGUST is a senior program officer at the National Research Council and study director for the Committee on Developing a Research Agenda on the Education of Limited English Proficient and Bilingual Students. Previously, she was a public school teacher and school administrator in California, a legislative assistant in the area of education for a U.S. Congressman from California, a grants officer for the Carnegie Corporation of New York, and director of education for the Children's Defense Fund. Dr. August has also worked as an educational consultant in evaluation and testing, program improvement, and federal and state education policy. She has a Ph.D. in education from Stanford University.

JAMES A. BANKS is professor of education and director of the Center for Multicultural Education at the University of Washington, Seattle. He is president-elect of the American Educational Research Association and is a past president of the National Council for the Social Studies. Professor Banks has written or edited 16 books in multicultural education and in social studies education, including *Teaching Strategies for Ethnic Studies; Multiethnic Education: Theory and Practice*; and *Multicultural Education, Transformative Knowledge, and Action*. He is the editor of the *Handbook of Research on Multicultural Education*, the first published research handbook in this field. Professor Banks has received four research awards from the American Educational Research Association and an honorary doctorate of humane letters (L.H.D.) from the Bank Street College of Education. He has a Ph.D. in social studies education from Michigan State University.

DONNA CHRISTIAN is president of the Center for Applied Linguistics in Washington, D.C., where she is active in research, program development and evaluation, and teacher education. She has also taught at the university level, including two years as a Fulbright senior lecturer in Poland. Her work has focused on the role of language in education, including second language education, dialect diversity, and policy issues. Dr. Christian has consulted and written extensively on these topics, including recent publications on issues of language and culture in school reform, the integration of language and content for immigrant students, and two-way bilingual education. She has an M.S. in applied linguistics and a Ph.D. in sociolinguistics from Georgetown University.

RICHARD DURÁN is professor in the Graduate School of Education at the University of California, Santa Barbara. Previously, he served as a research scientist at Educational Testing Service in Princeton. His fields of expertise include assessment and instruction of language minority students, and design and evaluation of interventions assisting language minority students. He is a member of the Technical Design Committee of New Standards and a member of various national technical panels that advise the National Center for Education Statistics on the conduct of surveys, including those on language-minority children. Professor Durán has a Ph.D. in psychology from the University of California at Berkeley, specializing in quantitative and cognitive psychology.

CARL F. KAESTLE is university professor of education, history, and public policy at Brown University. He is also senior fellow at the Annenberg Institute for School Reform at Brown University. Previously, he was a professor of education at the University of Chicago, and prior to that, a professor in the Departments of Educational Policy Studies and History at the University of Wisconsin-Madison, as well as chair of the Department of Educational Policy Studies and director of the Wisconsin Center for Educational Research. He has also been a high school teacher and a principal. He has written extensively on the history of education, the role of the federal government in education, and adult literacy. He has been a visiting fellow at the Charles Warren Center for Studies in American History at Harvard, the Shelby Cullom Davis Center for Historical Studies at Princeton and the Center for Advanced Study in the Behavioral Sciences. His current research interests combine history and policy—the area of reading, assessment, and adult literacy and the role of the federal government in elementary and secondary education. Dr. Kaestle is the current president of the National Academy of Education and has served on the advisory committee of the National Adult Literacy Survey. He is currently a member of the Board on Testing and Assessment of the National Research Council. He holds a Ph.D. in education from Harvard University.

DAVID KENNY is professor of psychology at the University of Connecticut. Previously, he taught at Harvard, was a fellow at the Center for Advanced Study in the Behavioral Sciences, and a visiting professor at Arizona State and Oxford University. His initial research area was in the analysis of non-experimental data and more recently, he has investigated person perception in naturalistic contexts. He has published 4 books and over 50 articles and chapters. Dr. Kenny served as first quantitative associate editor of *Psychological Bulletin* and is currently editor of the Guilford series *Methodology for the Social Sciences*. He has a Ph.D. in social psychology from Northwestern University.

GAEA LEINHARDT is senior scientist at the Learning Research and Development Center and professor of education at the University of Pittsburgh, where she directs the Instructional Explanations Project and chairs the Cognitive Studies in Education Program. Dr. Leinhardt began her career teaching in inner-city schools. Her research interests have focused on a combination of ethnographic and cognitive approaches to the fine-grained analysis of classroom phenomena and the analysis of cognitive aspects of teaching and learning in specific subject matter areas, such as mathematics, history, and geography. Currently, Dr. Leinhardt is developing a model of the cognitive structure of instructional explanations across subject matters, and developing portraits of teachers and students who are involved with educational restructuring programs. She has also been intensely involved in state and national efforts to improve teacher assessment. Dr. Leinhardt's work has won awards from the American Educational Research Association and the National Council for Geographic Education. She has a Ph.D. in educational research from the University of Pittsburgh.

ALBA ORTIZ is Ruben E. Hinojosa Regents professor in education, associate dean for academic affairs and research in the College of Education at the University of Texas at Austin, professor and director of bilingual special education in the Department of Special Education, and director of the Office of Bilingual Education in the College of Education. Previously, she served as a speech, hearing, and language therapist in the San Antonio school district and as an instructional consultant and materials specialist for special education and migrant education in San Antonio. Prior to that, she was assistant professor of Special Education and Director of the Bilingual/Bicultural Education at San Jose State University and assistant professor and director of Bilingual Chicano Studies at Southern Methodist University. She is past president of the International Council for Exceptional Children. Dr. Ortiz is a frequent presenter and invited speaker at local, state, and national meetings and conferences on topics related to special education and bilingual education and has published extensively on these topics. She has a Ph.D. in special education administration from the University of Texas at Austin.

LUCINDA PEASE-ALVAREZ is associate professor of education at the University of California, Santa Cruz. She has a varied background working with language-minority students as a teacher and researcher and has taught in bilingual and ESL (English-as-a-second-language) programs at both the primary and secondary level. As a teacher educator, she teaches courses on literacy development, bilingualism, and first- and second-language acquisition. Dr. Pease-Alvarez's research interests include children's uses of oral and written language in home, school, and community settings. She is currently involved in a multifaceted longitudinal study of native-language maintenance and shift toward English in bilingual children of Mexican descent. She is coauthor of *Pushing Boundaries: Language Learning and Socialization in a Mexicano Community*, which focuses on the language practices and perspectives of children and adults living in a Mexican immigrant community. She has a Ph.D. in education from Stanford.

CATHERINE SNOW is Henry Lee Shattuck professor of education at the Harvard Graduate School of Education. She is also codirector of the Home-School Study on Language and Literacy Development, a longitudinal study of literacy development. She has served as acting dean of the Harvard Graduate School of Education and is currently chair of the Department of Human Development and Psychology. Dr. Snow's early research focused on the features of children's social and linguistic environments that facilitated language development, on cross-cultural differences in mother-child interaction, and on factors affecting second language acquisition. She has done research on the factors affecting the acquisition of literacy and on relations between aspects of oral language development and later literacy achievement in both monolingual and bilingual children. Dr. Snow edits *Applied Psycholinguistics*, serves on the editorial staff of numerous journals, and has consulted and written extensively on a range of language development issues. She has a Ph.D. in psychology from McGill University.

DEBORAH STIPEK is professor in the Department of Education at the University of California, Los Angeles, and director of the UCLA laboratory school (Seeds, University Elementary School), and of the UCLA Urban Education Studies Center. She is also a member of the MacArthur Foundation Network on Successful Pathways in Middle Childhood. Dr. Stipek's research interests focus on the effect of classroom contexts and instruction on children's motivation and learning. She has done many studies on cognitions and emotions associated with motivation in academic settings, and her recent work has concentrated on early childhood education and the transition into school. She has a Ph.D. in developmental psychology from Yale.

OTHER REPORTS FROM THE BOARD ON CHILDREN, YOUTH, AND FAMILIES

New Findings on Poverty and Child Health and Nutrition: Summary of a Research Briefing (1998)

Violence in Families: Assessing Prevention and Treatment Programs (1998)

Improving Schooling for Language-Minority Students: A Research Agenda (1997)

New Findings on Welfare and Children's Development: Summary of a Research Briefing (1997)

Youth Development and Neighborhood Influences: Challenges and Opportunities: Summary of a Workshop (1996)

Paying Attention to Children in a Changing Health Care System: Summaries of Workshops (with the Board on Health Promotion and Disease Prevention of the Institute of Medicine) (1996)

Beyond the Blueprint: Directions for Research on Head Start's Families: Report of Three Roundtable Meetings (1996)

Child Care for Low-Income Families: Directions for Research: Summary of a Workshop (1996)

Service Provider Perspectives on Family Violence Interventions: Proceedings of a Workshop (1995)

"Immigrant Children and Their Families: Issues for Research and Policy" in *The Future of Children* (1995)

Integrating Federal Statistics on Children (with the Committee on National Statistics of the National Research Council) (1995)

Child Care for Low-Income Families: Summary of Two Workshops (1995)

New Findings on Children, Families, and Economic Self-Sufficiency: Summary of a Research Briefing (1995)

The Impact of War on Child Health in the Countries of the Former Yugoslavia: A Workshop Summary (with the Institute of Medicine and the Office of International Affairs of the National Research Council) (1995)

Cultural Diversity and Early Education: Report of a Workshop (1994)

Benefits and Systems of Care for Maternal and Child Health: Workshop Highlights (with the Board on Health Promotion and Disease Prevention of the Institute of Medicine) (1994)

Protecting and Improving the Quality of Children Under Health Care Reform: Workshop Highlights (with the Board on Health Promotion and Disease Prevention of the Institute of Medicine) (1994)

America's Fathers and Public Policy: Report of a Workshop (1994)

Violence and the American Family: Report of a Workshop (1994)